THE ONLY
LEADERS
WORTH* FOLLOWING

THE ONLY
LEADERS
WORTH* FOLLOWING

Why some leaders succeed, others fail,
and how the quality of our lives hangs in the balance

TIM SPIKER

The Aperio Press
atlanta

Published by The Aperio
www.TheAperio.com

Spiker, Tim, 1972-
The only leaders worth following: why some leaders succeed, others fail, and how the quality of our lives hangs in the balance / Tim Spiker.
— 2nd edition
ISBN 978-1-950867-04-2

TheAperio.com

*To everyone who wants to be led well
and everyone who wants to be worth following*

Contents

FOREWORD

It has long been held that leadership is all about execution. Leaders set direction and strategy, determine resource allocation, and develop talent while motivating the troops. Historically, these skills set the table for most leadership curricula. To be sure, they are critical skills that can't be ignored, but they exclude one simple truth: leaders cast far more than a strategic web. They project themselves onto and into everything and everyone they lead.

The *Who* of leadership reveals itself not in what leaders say (though that is important), but in what they value, where they focus, and how they treat the most vulnerable people on the team. It even shows up in the balance of inclusion versus exclusion that characterizes the leader's organizational habits.

The *Who* of leadership is often obscured by ambiguity, imprecision, and uncertainty. It seldom lends itself to precise measurement. Its applications can vary widely based on individual leaders' circumstances, capabilities, and capacities. There are no action lists to apply and no handy formulas to use. Instead, there are principles to explore that challenge conventional notions of the relationship between leaders, followers, and the endeavors they pursue.

More than 30 years ago, I was asked to journey down the road of personal development that shaped the *Who* of my leadership. My guide suggested that the same person acting in the same ways would fail identically to how I had failed in the past. So I was asked to change . . . and to do so as quickly as possible. Pulling it off required acceptance, faith, courage, and vulnerability. Though my journey is neither perfect nor complete, I can tell you from personal experience that it has been well worth the effort. If you choose to pursue growth in the *Who* of your leadership, I believe you'll find it worth the effort as well.

In this book, Tim Spiker launches leaders into a developmental journey similar to the one I began 30 years ago. In *The Only Leaders Worth* Following*, he explains the *Who* Not What Principle* and in doing so captures the essence of the tension between leadership and followership. Based on a broad consultancy as well as organizational and hands-on experience, Tim pulls together the crucial but almost subliminal leadership qualities required to find "Whoville" (with a bow to the genius of author Theodor Seuss Geisel). This is where effective leadership flourishes based on its understanding of the roles that fear and trust play in personal and organizational performance. Leaders who learn and apply these truths to themselves will release the type of discretionary effort that is only seen when followers are engaged and unafraid.

For 48 months, Tim worked directly with Boral's Global Executive Committee taking them through the content of his *Who* Not What* leadership methodology. This has included offsite deep dives with Boral's top 100 executives discovering the impact of worldview on our outlook, judgments, and most profoundly our interpretation of the world as it presents itself through our lenses. He and his team have engaged multiple division leaders and their teams from Sydney to Singapore to Atlanta providing insight into the power of being Others

Focused once you are Inwardly Sound. These, of course, are terms of art that require detailed reflection and exposition . . . and a guide for the uninitiated.

This content is not for the faint of heart. It requires a long hard look at the imperfection that is the stuff of "us"—not perfect, broken in parts, mending in others, but trying and at times getting it right. We are best judged, of course, by our followers, not ourselves.

I have known Tim for over 15 years as a colleague and friend. He continues to teach me about important things in life. Our dialogue on the human condition will, I hope, follow me to my grave. Let him lead you for a while and see if his insights can help inform who you are and, in doing so, help you reach your potential as a leader.

MIKE KANE

Husband to Kathleen; Father of McHenry, Padraic, Heather, Anna, James, and Daniel; Grandfather of Brendan, Cathan, Kieran, Claire, and Tessie; Son, Brother, and Friend;

and also,

Chief Executive Officer and Managing Director
Boral Limited
North Sydney, Australia

At the time of publication, Boral Limited has a market capitalization of more than $4 billion (USD) created through more than 600 operating sites in 17 countries and over 20,000 employees and permanent contractors. Boral is the largest construction materials company in Australia, the largest gypsum company in Asia, and the largest specialty coal combustion product, exterior tile, and cladding business in North America.

"It can even be a single note which defines the entire song."
LEON REDBONE

INTRODUCTION

I'd just moved into a new office in my company's Southeastern U.S. headquarters in Atlanta. It was a nondescript room with neutral-colored paint, a coordinated desk and filing cabinet, and a tall skinny window looking out on the parking lot. There was nothing on the walls yet, save that most essential and splendid of all office items: the whiteboard.

Drawn on that whiteboard was a graphical depiction of leadership. Some people snuggle up with a good book. Others settle in to watch a well-directed movie. I get cozy with leadership models. Not many people spend their afternoons doing such a thing. Truth is, I wasn't supposed to be doing that either. I was supposed to be working on a weekly report. But there I was instead, doing what I'd done for most of my professional life: pondering leadership.

I gazed at the circles, lines, and words in that diagram. I'd discussed and debated them with many colleagues over the years. I stared and thought and thought and stared. I wasn't a sleuth attempting to solve a mystery. I wasn't trying to uncover a new insight. I was just thinking. And then the insight found me. It hit me as clearly as hearing a single note on a piano—a strong, resonant middle C. It felt as if a divine message had arrived simultaneously in my gut, heart, head, and soul. It was simple. It had been true all along. How had I not seen it before?

I rushed down the hall to my mentor's office. It was fitting to be in his presence at this moment. He, more than anyone else I'd ever worked for, encouraged me to press forward in this work even when my efforts were complicated and clumsy. I scribbled on his whiteboard as quickly as I could, my hands unable to keep up with the ideas in my head. My arrows and lines were drawn so sloppily they could have passed for modern art. I concluded the flurry of drawing and writing with the divine message that had struck the whole of myself. I spoke it rather than writing it. It was three simple words: *Who* Not What.*

I didn't invent the *Who* Not What Principle* any more than I invented gravity. It simply is. And just like gravity, *Who* Not What* has affected every person in every country in every age since the beginning of time. It is a seminal truth within leadership. The reach of *Who* Not What* extends as far and wide as the impact of leadership itself. And it does so whether we're conscious of it or not. We are hit squarely and tangibly by the reality of *Who* Not What* in our lives each and every day.

Yet we rarely talk about it.

It's my vocational calling to pull back the curtain on *Who* Not What*—to expose its hidden existence, identify the masks it wears, and foster dialogue about it. In doing so, I hope to enable leaders and followers alike to experience better leadership, better results, and better lives.

Please know in advance that this is not a how-to book. Not because there aren't methods and practices available to help us become more effective leaders, but because I want us to stay focused on understanding these concepts in depth. Moving too quickly to "how-to" diminishes the long-term impact of the truths presented because it lessens the depth of our understanding of them. So for now, put away the to-do lists and checkboxes and give yourself the freedom to immerse yourself deeply in understanding every aspect and nuance of the *Who* Not What Principle*.

As you read, take a look for yourself. Consider your own experiences and test if *Who* Not What* accounts for much of what you've seen, heard, and experienced about leadership. If it does (and I have no doubt it will), it will then be your turn to share the truth of *Who* Not What* with others and leverage it in your own life as well.

Ti

Tim Spiker

"Intuition will tell the thinking mind where to look next."

JONAS SALK

CHAPTER ONE

You Already Know

WHAT YOUR GUT-LEVEL INTUITION ALREADY UNDERSTANDS
ABOUT LEADERSHIP AND THE *WHO* NOT WHAT PRINCIPLE*

Let's begin by putting the most important idea in this book on the table right here and right now. If you remember nothing else from this book, please (as in, I'm begging you) remember this next statement:

*3/4 OF YOUR EFFECTIVENESS AS A LEADER COMES FROM WHO YOU ARE, NOT WHAT YOU DO

This is the *Who* Not What Principle*. It explains why some leaders reach their potential while other leaders don't. It tells us why some leaders help create fulfilling lives for those they lead while other leaders suck the life out of their followers. It clarifies why some leaders consistently achieve bottom-line results while so many other leaders can't. In short, *Who* Not What* tells us who's worth following and who isn't.

After 15 years of studying leadership, I'm convinced the principle of *Who* Not What* is the single most important truth about leadership. It also happens to be one of the most under-appreciated, and therefore neglected, truths about leadership.

When you read "3/4 of your effectiveness as a leader comes from who you are, not what you do," I don't know whether your defenses went up, your spirit said, "Yes!" or you wondered, "Could that possibly be true?" Regardless, what follows is a series of real-life examples, psychology, and data (yes, data!) that reveal that the single greatest determiner of our success and failure as leaders is how well developed we are as people. We'll investigate what it means to be a well-developed *Who*. (Spoiler alert: It's about a whole lot more than having good character.) We'll also explore a metaphor for leadership that displays how *Who* Not What* influences every action a leader takes. We'll finish by addressing common misunderstandings about *Who* Not What* and WIIFY . . . ATROTW (What's In It For You . . . And The Rest Of The World) when you understand and apply this truth about leadership.

Footnotes, by their very nature, do not take center stage. They live in the background even as they shape and support the conclusions we come to. Likewise is the relationship between the *Who* Not What Principle* and leadership. So I've decided to leverage the footnote concept to help us stay conscious of the *Who* Not What Principle*. On the front cover of this book beside the word "worth" and throughout its pages, you will see numerous aster-isks. Each one is a visual cue to remember that the *Who* Not What Principle* is at work behind the scenes in every leadership story. *Who* is what makes us worth (or not worth) following.

The leaders chronicled in this book run the gamut from extremely effective to grossly deficient. Please note that I routinely alter the specifics of their stories—names of people and companies, genders, industries, departments, job titles, locations—to maintain anonymity wherever appropriate. I change only the inconsequential particulars of these stories. Their substance and critical details have been preserved as valuable examples from which to learn.[1]

MY STORY

If you're the type of person that requires statistically significant evidence to begin exploration of a concept or idea, I encourage you to jump to Chapter 3 and start there. Once you've consumed the data there, come back to read Chapters 1 and 2. For everyone else, our first step on this journey is for you to see that you don't have to study leadership for decades to see the truth of *Who* Not What*. You already understand it. You intuitively recognize it as soon as you have an opportunity to see who a leader is as a person. To illustrate this, let's dive into a leadership story that's personal to me.

I'd just landed what I considered to be my dream job 10 to 15 years earlier in life than I'd thought possible. I was excited as I packed up my car to leave Phoenix, Arizona, to work for the marketing and brand management division of a technology firm based in Charlotte, North Carolina. But within six months of the move, my excitement was gone. I loved the content of my work, but life was difficult within the company. Dysfunction and poor communication reigned. Numerous talented colleagues left or planned to leave. The corporate environment felt toxic, especially in our division. In three short years that felt like three *long* years, no fewer than five different people led our team.

*3/4 OF YOUR EFFECTIVENESS AS A LEADER COMES FROM WHO YOU ARE, NOT WHAT YOU DO

A TALE OF TWO LEADERS

Of those five leaders, Martin and Dave created a dichotomy that put *Who* * *Not What* on clear display. One of them turned out to be the best leader for whom I've ever worked. The other was . . . well . . . he was closer to the opposite end of the spectrum. They led me in virtually identical environments: same company, culture, colleagues, projects, and economic conditions. The only variable was who was leading me. It was the perfect experiment to answer the question, "How much difference does a leader make?"

Rather than me telling you who the better leader was between Martin and Dave, let's play a game. Table 1 (below) contains

Martin	Dave
Political Science, United States Naval Academy	Liberal Arts, Northern Iowa University
Master of Philosophy, Baylor University	JD, Loyola (Chicago) University, School of Law
Managing Director, Boutique Marketing Firm	South American Division Executive VP, International Chemicals Company
Exceptional at convincing his constituents to buy into his ideas	Expert in value creation through deals (acquisitions, divestitures, joint ventures, and negotiations)
Excellent public speaker and an acceptable business strategist	Excellent business strategist and acceptable public speaker

Table 1: Martin vs. Dave

selections from Martin's and Dave's résumés. Read these and then guess which leader was not only the best leader I've ever worked for, but also one of the best leaders I've observed in all of my years of leadership consulting and coaching.

So, what's your guess? Who was the exceptional leader? This isn't a rhetorical question. I really want you to guess. Actually, don't just guess. Let's do one other thing as well. After choosing Martin or Dave, indicate on the scale below (Figure 1) how sure you are of your answer. Don't skip logging this piece of information. It's a critical part of what comes next.

Figure 1: *Who Was the Exceptional Leader?*

The late commentator Paul Harvey was famous for offering intriguing, improbable opening lines. The titles and first few sentences of his radio stories made listeners think, "How on earth could that be true?" Then Harvey would say, "And now, the rest of the story." In the minutes that followed, he would tell the full story, weaving its nuances until his unbelievable opening lines morphed into the only plausible explanation for what had happened. Harvey left his listeners thinking, "Now I get it. It all makes sense."

And now, the rest of *my* story.

In the table that follows (Table 2) you'll find more details about Martin and Dave. These are real experiences with and observations of each leader.

Martin	Dave
During my first week of employment, Martin left me to manage a room full of potential clients—company presidents, no less—whom I had just met. He returned 15 minutes later and whispered in my ear, "That's all the development you'll ever get from me."	After stepping into leadership of the division, Dave immediately ascertained I was unhappy and requested a meeting to hear my concerns and frustrations.
Martin required me to cancel a vacation the day before it began—I'd scheduled it a year in advance—because he wanted me to fix a miscommunication issue for which he was the primary player. Before the week ended, he forgot I'd canceled my vacation to resolve the issue.	Rather than passing pressure down the chain of command as senior leaders placed it on him, Dave absorbed it. This created space for his subordinates to do their best work, unfettered by the pressure and politics of the organization. He did this without concern for how it might negatively impact his compensation and upward mobility within the firm.
Martin didn't once admit fault or contribution to any difficulties within the division or with our constituents.	Dave had a clear under-standing of his personal shortcomings and shared them with the team.
Martin routinely got excited about the magnitude of potential revenue from new customers but rarely displayed passion for the art and craft of our work.	When offered a job opportunity outside the company that perfectly fit his talents and experience, Dave called me to ensure I would be okay if he left the company.

Table 2: Martin vs. Dave—The Rest of the Story

Now guess again who the exceptional leader was. Then, just as you did the first time around, indicate how sure you are of your answer on the scale below (Figure 2). If you tend to be suspicious, let me assure you this is not a trick question.

Figure 2: Who Was the Exceptional Leader?—Round #2

Who did you choose as the exceptional leader this time? We both know you chose Dave as the exceptional leader. And you're correct. He was the exceptional leader. Not only are you correct, but if you're like most people, your confidence in your answer was also much higher the second time around. This displays two things:

1. The truth of *Who* Not What*
2. Your intuitive understanding of its existence

When people see the first table, they're divided about whether Martin or Dave was the exceptional leader, and confidence in those guesses tends toward the "I'm totally guessing" section of the scale. But after "the rest of the story," nearly everyone identifies Dave as the exceptional leader, and they do so with an extremely high level of confidence in their answers.

---

*3/4 OF YOUR EFFECTIVENESS AS A LEADER COMES FROM WHO YOU ARE, NOT WHAT YOU DO

The first table lists titles, education, and skills—things we often associate with effective leadership. But it didn't tell you definitively whether Dave or Martin was the better leader, did it? The second table reveals a little bit about who Dave and Martin were as people. And that made all the difference in helping you decide.

THE QUALITIES OF A GREAT LEADER

If you were to create a list of qualities to describe Dave as a person based on the second table, your list might include emotional maturity, compassion, security (as opposed to insecurity), willingness to sacrifice on behalf of others, thoughtfulness, humility, and transparency. An identical exercise with Martin might include self-centeredness, inconsiderateness, greed, lack of self-awareness, and insecurity.

But you didn't need to make a list weighing the attributes of Martin and Dave to know who you'd rather follow. You understood intuitively who the better leader was once you knew who the more well-developed person was. We know in our guts who we'd run through the proverbial wall for and who we wouldn't. You don't have to read a book about leadership to know that Dave was the better leader.

I still remember the first one-on-one conversation I had with Dave. We had a division meeting where he was introduced as our new leader. After the usual project review conversations, Dave asked to meet with me about a key project.

About 37 seconds into the conversation he said, "We can talk about the project stuff later. Tell me, how frustrated are you?"

By the end of that conversation, I knew Dave was a man worthy of trust. I decided to share with him something I hadn't shared with anyone else: I was in the process of updating my résumé. I planned to begin a job search within a couple of weeks. I also told him that in order to endure the current situation, I'd need more money. Dave asked me to hold off on looking for a new job for a couple of months and told me he'd look into the raise. He asked me to give him a chance to make some changes. I agreed.

What ensued was a massive change for me as a follower. In just 60 days, Dave created an entirely different atmosphere within the division. He shared who he was, faults and all. He openly encouraged the group regarding the work we did. And he did all that while maintaining a high value on quality work and profits. Over the course of those 60 days and the months that

YOU UNDERSTOOD INTUITIVELY WHO THE BETTER LEADER WAS ONCE YOU KNEW WHO THE MORE WELL-DEVELOPED PERSON WAS.

followed, can you guess what happened to my need for more money? It disappeared. It turns out, more money wasn't what I needed. What I needed was a better leader.

For the year that followed, I reported to Dave and enjoyed my work exponentially more than I had in my first year at the company. Then, one evening, I got a call from Dave. He was seriously considering a job offer and wanted to talk to me about it. His description of the opportunity sounded tailor-made for him—a familiar industry, a major leadership role, and significantly improved compensation. It was obvious he should take it. So why was he calling me? He wanted to make sure I'd be okay if he took the job. That's right. Knowing how much internal

*3/4 OF YOUR EFFECTIVENESS AS A LEADER COMES FROM WHO YOU ARE, NOT WHAT YOU DO

support he was giving me behind the scenes, he wanted to make sure *I* would be okay if he left. That's the kind of person Dave was. He's still that kind of person today. That's the kind of leader for whom people run through walls. And that's something you intuitively understood when you learned a little bit about who Dave was as a person.

So you've now been introduced to the principle of *Who* * *Not What* and your intuitive ability to recognize its importance in leadership. But let's not stop with my experiences. Every person I have ever worked with has stories both good and bad that point to the existence of *Who* * *Not What*. That's why we're now going to switch gears and focus on you. Let's take a look at how your experiences as a follower point to the truth of *Who* * *Not What*.

*"The human heart feels things the eyes cannot see,
and knows what the mind cannot understand."*

ROBERT VALETT

CHAPTER TWO

Heartfelt

HOW YOU HAVE FELT THE IMPACT OF *WHO* NOT WHAT*
IN YOUR EXPERIENCES AS A FOLLOWER

I'm not the only one who has experienced the truth of *Who* Not What.* You have, too. To show you how, let's do a survey with a sample size of one (that one would be you). Take a few minutes to make a list of the best leaders you have personally followed. Most people write down between one and three names. If you've been blessed to follow many great leaders, limit your list to your top five. Ready? Go.

1. _____
2. _____
3. _____
4. _____
5. _____

If you're like many people, your list included the names of bosses early in your career, parents, high school teachers, middle school sports coaches, aunts, uncles, clergy, and college advisors.

But *why* did you choose those particular leaders? Was it because of their stalwart strategic capabilities or their excellence in producing quarterly results or their skill in scheduling and project planning? Probably not. If you look below the surface, you'll see that those leaders took the time to care about you. They selflessly invested in you. They were authentic and honest with you. They cared more about what they were giving to the relationship than what they could get from it. You wrote down those names because of who those people were to you.

These are your *Who* * *Not What* stories.

COACH SHONDA

I was once facilitating an exercise with a couple hundred people. It was similar to the one I just asked you to do. I gave each person in the room five minutes to share with two other people at their tables about a leader that had personally and positively impacted them. As they began to share with one another, the energy level in the room rose tangibly. Their quiet discussions grew into a din.

As they finished the exercise, I asked for volunteers to share a few stories. One employee named Makaila spoke about Coach Shonda, her high school basketball coach. Coach Shonda had experienced a storied coaching career. State championships and consistently high performing teams were the norm. As Makaila described her coach's approach to basketball, it appeared on the surface that Coach Shonda knew a lot about two things: (1) basketball and (2) motivating high school girls.

But as Makaila continued to describe Coach Shonda, the focus of her comments shifted. Makaila began to speak about Coach Shonda's humility and genuine care for her players. It became clearer and clearer that what landed Coach Shonda on Makaila's list wasn't her strategic mind or rah-rah speeches, but her heart and soul. In a not-so-surprising twist, Coach Shonda's love for her players was the very thing that enabled her to push them hard toward success without producing rebellion or resentment.

Makaila's story isn't unique. Time and again when I ask people to reach into their pasts to identify the leaders who have most positively impacted them, the truth of *Who* Not What* comes out. The conversations start out about successes, strategies, and techniques. But we don't stay there. Inevitably, the inner qualities of our "All-Time Best Leaders" shine through as the true drivers of their leadership success. And all in attendance nod their heads in understanding.

When we work for well-developed people who carry inside them the best humanity is capable of, we *feel* the difference. You do. I do. We all do.

JUAN'S CRISIS

I knew an up-and-coming leader named Juan. Juan had everything going for him in a large, prestigious marketing firm in New York City. He had a history of leading successful projects, was working for an outstanding boss, and was on track to one day become a top leader in the company.

One day Juan received a call from Suyin, a former colleague at the firm. Suyin had branched out to start her own marketing firm four years earlier in the trendy city of Austin, Texas. The first years of Suyin's new venture had gone well and her company was starting to hit critical mass. She needed a strong leader who understood the internal operations of a well-run

---

*3/4 OF YOUR EFFECTIVENESS AS A LEADER COMES FROM WHO YOU ARE, NOT WHAT YOU DO

marketing agency. Suyin wanted Juan to join her as her new Chief Operations Officer. Juan had a positive history with Suyin that included closely-aligned values. With a desire to help build something nearly from the ground floor up, Juan decided to join Suyin.

Within 15 months of moving to Austin, Juan's leap had become a full-fledged free fall. Suyin hadn't been in a position of significant leadership when she and Juan worked together previously. Now that she was, Juan saw a different side of Suyin. Suyin took small pieces of information and made inaccurate assumptions about Juan's motives and character, which included believing Juan was intentionally trying to undermine Suyin's authority and leadership within the company. Suyin's fears, rather than Suyin herself, seemed to be leading the company. It was stunning to Juan.

WE FEEL THE DIFFERENCE BETWEEN FOLLOWING WHOLE, WELL-DEVELOPED PEOPLE AND FOLLOWING THOSE WHO AREN'T.

Juan called me in the midst of his crisis. His pain and frustration were evident. Juan isn't a guy normally given to overt emotion, but the magnitude of how his life was affected by Suyin's leadership was so great he was brought to tears a number of times while sharing his situation with me. I heard his sadness and felt for him unlike any other leader with whom I'd ever interacted.

In his dark professional moment, Juan wasn't listening to his gut-level intuition about *Who* * *Not What*. He was *feeling* the impact of it. Profoundly and personally, he felt what it was like to follow a fearful and suspicious leader. Just as I felt the positive swing of following a healthy, well-developed leader in Dave, Juan felt the opposite in following Suyin.

The repercussions weren't limited to the realm of feelings and emotions. Juan decided there was only one sane course of action in response to his experience: He resigned and moved on. In the end, Juan wasn't the only one who paid the price for Suyin's lack of development as a person. So did everyone within Suyin's organization, including Suyin herself. They lost the opportunity to work with and for Juan, an immensely talented and high-potential leader.

We don't just intuit *Who* Not What* in our guts. We feel it with our hearts. When underdeveloped people lead us, their lack of wholeness affects us as followers. And when we follow leaders who have done the hard work of becoming whole people, we feel that as well.

But the truth of *Who* Not What* is not confined to personal experiences, emotions, and intuition. It's more robust than that. There's data to back it up. Let's break out our calculators and crunch the numbers.

*3/4 OF YOUR EFFECTIVENESS AS A LEADER COMES FROM WHO YOU ARE, NOT WHAT YOU DO

"Most discoveries even today are a combination of serendipity and of searching."

SIDDHARTHA MUKHERJEE

CHAPTER THREE

Stumbling Into Significance

ACCIDENTALLY DISCOVERED DATA THAT POINTS
TO THE REALITY OF *WHO* NOT WHAT*

Early in my career I was part of a consulting group that brought executives and other leaders to the west side of Pikes Peak for a week-long leader development experience. The picturesque setting and spotty cell phone coverage were perfect for getting professionals out of their everyday atmospheres so they could fully contemplate and evaluate themselves as leaders.

A critical component of the experience was a set of assessments. One was a leadership assessment that gave participants both quantitative and qualitative opportunities to hear how subordinates, peers, superiors, and others experienced them as leaders. These assessments are called "360s" because they give feedback from 360 degrees around the leader. Accompanying the leadership 360 was an assessment that measured natural abilities and another that focused on personality style.

Participants routinely asked our consultants questions like,

"Is there a particular personality profile that produces better leadership? Is there a set of natural abilities that enables leaders to perform better than others who don't have them? Is there a way for us to use assessments to predict which leaders have the highest probability of becoming exceptional leaders?"

Over the years, our firm had collected a couple thousand data points through these assessments—more than enough to investigate our clients' questions with statistical integrity. So we decided to run the numbers. I fully expected to find a valuable correlation. As it turned out, I was right . . . and wrong. We found something huge. But we found it by accident. And we didn't find it where we thought we would.

The leadership 360 measured our clients in eight categories of leadership. Influenced and informed by leadership experts such as Warren Bennis, Robert Greenleaf, and John Kotter, these categories represented a broad set of leadership principles that applied to any leader at any level of an organization.

They were:[1]
- Set Direction
- Think Strategically
- Align Resources
- Motivate and Inspire
- Others Focused
- Execute and Follow Through
- Inwardly Sound
- Develop Talent

If we assume that these eight areas of leadership carry equal importance, we'd expect each area to account for 12.5% of the variability in a leader's performance on the 360 assessment. Any two areas of leadership should account for 25% of a leader's performance. But what we found was quite different.

AN UNEXPECTED RESULT

Armed with graduate-level experience in statistical analysis and a degree in Industrial Organizational Psychology, our resident number cruncher, Vanessa Kiley, took more than 2,000 data points and commanded the SPSS software to do its thing.

I still remember the night I sat down to talk with Vanessa about the results of her analysis.

"So, what did you find?" I asked.

"Nothing," Vanessa said.

"Nothing? Really? No correlations at all?"

"Nothing," Vanessa said. "There is no statistically significant data to suggest any particular personality trait or natural ability or any combination of personality traits and natural abilities creates better leaders overall or better results in any particular aspect of leadership." She took a deep breath and said again, "Nothing."

"Well, at least we know," I said.

ACCORDING TO RESEARCH DATA, THERE ARE NO NATURAL ABILITIES OR PERSONALITY STYLES THAT AUTOMATICALLY MAKE LEADERS MORE EFFECTIVE.

I was surprisingly satisfied with the results despite my expectation that we'd find some kind of correlation. At least now I'd be able to quickly and confidently give our clients a statistically verifiable answer. I immediately began looking forward to the next time one of our clients posed one of those common questions. There was no personality profile that led to better leadership. No secret code of human DNA that created better leaders. No magic combination to unlock the door of successful leadership.

---

*3/4 OF YOUR EFFECTIVENESS AS A LEADER COMES FROM WHO YOU ARE, NOT WHAT YOU DO

I stood up, turned around, and started to walk out of Vanessa's office. And then she spoke up.

"But I did find one other thing."

I turned around. "Oh yeah, what's that?"

"I found that nearly 70% of the variability in the leadership 360s is driven by just two aspects of leadership."

"What?" I said as I walked back into her office and sat down nearly breathless. "Which two?"

THE BIG REVEAL

Vanessa made the answer public in July 2008 when, armed with over 20,000 data points and a second pass at the analysis, she published the results in the company's quarterly publication (Figure 3).[2] As the volume of data points grew from just over 2,000 to more than 20,000, the impact of the two most influential leadership categories climbed from just under 70% to 77%. The influence of these two categories on a leader's performance was even bigger than we'd originally discovered. It now exceeded by more than three times the 25% influence you'd expect to see from any two categories if each of the eight leadership categories were equally important.

So which two categories were driving over 3/4 of a leader's effectiveness?

INWARDLY SOUND & OTHERS FOCUSED

In her article, Vanessa described the qualities that live within these two areas. Ideals such as personal disciplines, integrity, authenticity, health in all areas of life, self-awareness, a clearly understood sense of purpose, humility, emotional intelligence, and unconditional love all made the list. Such ideals are the foundation of what makes a well-developed human being. Apparently, they were also the foundation of what makes leaders exceptional.

The study's conclusion was simple and unambiguous: well-developed people make more effective leaders.

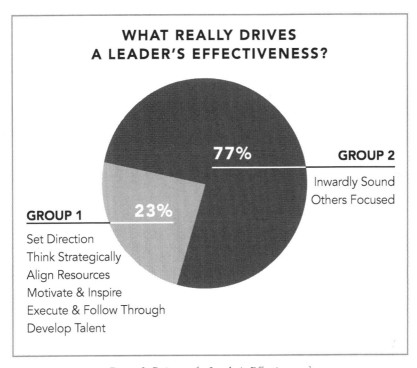

Figure 3: Drivers of a Leader's Effectiveness [3]

This was extraordinary stuff. But somehow, this discovery got buried. What should've been "Extra! Extra! Read all about it!" news ended up living on page 24 of the publication. Vanessa's article had no visual header to speak of and limited graphics. It didn't even qualify as a feature story. If you thumbed through the magazine, it would have been easy to miss it.

Why wasn't it given more attention? I really don't know. Maybe it was too far outside normal leadership thinking. For some, its uniqueness may have been too scary to champion. What was revelatory and statistically provable ended up languishing in obscurity even within the very publication in which it was printed. Like having an original Monet under a dust cloth in the attic, this priceless information sat hidden away and out of sight. Thankfully, there were **THE STUDY'S CONCLUSION WAS SIMPLE AND UNAMBIGUOUS: WELL-DEVELOPED PEOPLE MAKE MORE EFFECTIVE LEADERS.** others who were willing to pull this information out of the shadows and put it on display for the entire world to see.

MORE EVIDENCE

A few years ago, the *Harvard Business Review* published the results of a study by KRW International, a leadership consultancy based in the United States.[4] The study, led by KRW founder Fred Kiel, was created to determine if the positive inner qualities of leaders produce better bottom-line results.

Using anonymous follower ratings, Kiel and his associates calculated the quality of CEOs and their senior teams on integrity, responsibility, forgiveness, and compassion and then compared those ratings to each organization's financial performance (Figure 4). They found that the bottom 10 CEOs and senior leadership teams as measured on integrity, responsibility, forgiveness, and compassion experienced a return on assets (ROA) of 1.93% where the top 10 CEOs and senior leadership teams as measured on those same qualities experienced an ROA of 9.35%.[5,6] That's nearly a 400% increase in ROA. Said Kiel, "I was unprepared to discover how robust the connection really is."[7]

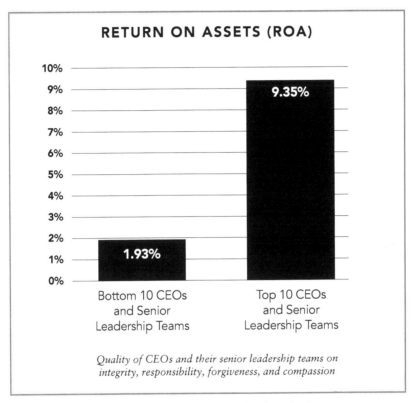

Figure 4: ROA and Well-Developed Leaders [8]

I have to admit my eyes popped out just a little bit when I first discovered KRW had the boldness to rate leaders on those four qualities, most especially on forgiveness and compassion. These simply aren't concepts regularly discussed alongside financial performance. I was further entranced when I saw that KRW's four characteristics precisely aligned with the categories of Inwardly Sound (integrity and responsibility) and Others Focused (forgiveness and compassion). Without any coordination or collaboration, we were singing off the same sheet of music as KRW.

2,000,000 CONFIRMATIONS

I had the good fortune of being introduced to David Byrum, a Senior Consultant at Human Synergistics Australia. (Human Synergistics Australia is part of the Human Synergistics International Group. The company is known on multiple continents for its research and unique developmental exercises.) David and I had a common client. Through that client David got exposed to the *Who* Not What Principle*. We met in Chicago to discuss how our work might fit together.

In rather short order, I learned from David that Human Synergistics had a treasure trove of data that pointed directly to the reality of *Who* Not What*. During the 1970s, Dr. J. Clayton Lafferty, founder of Human Synergistics, along with Dr. Robert A. Cooke of the University of Michigan, created the Life Styles Inventory™ (LSI). Though originally created to help individuals maximize the quality of their own lives, the LSI uncovered meaningful insights regarding leadership effectiveness.

Data from the LSI found a statistical correlation between what Human Synergistics calls "Constructive Styles" and leadership effectiveness (Figure 5). In Australia, where David consults, they found that leaders with the most constructive styles (top 10%) outperform leaders with the least constructive styles (bottom 10%) in what Human Synergistics identifies as three important aspects of leadership:[9]

+ 33% task effectiveness
+ 33% quality of relationships
+ 38% overall effectiveness

Human Synergistics went on to create two new leadership-focused assessments, each of which produced compelling data that further connected the Constructive Styles to leadership effectiveness.[10]

Naturally, my primary question for David was about what comprises the Constructive Styles. He shared that the Constructive Styles are made up of behaviors that encourage leaders to be comfortable with who they are as people, establish and achieve goals, support and develop others, and cooperate with and seek the views of others. These ideals are strikingly similar to what it means to be Inwardly Sound and Others Focused.

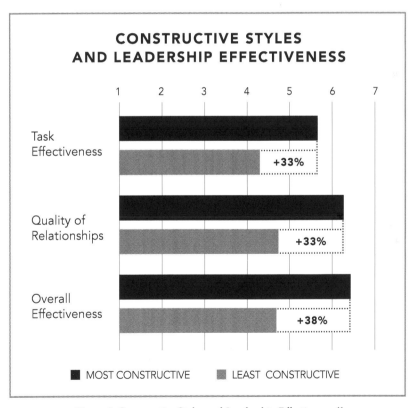

Figure 5: Constructive Styles and Leadership Effectiveness [11]

Said David, "When I read about the data that pointed toward *Who* Not What*, I felt like I was reading our [Human Synergistics] data. The similarities were uncanny. When leaders are truly Constructive—or in your vernacular Inwardly Sound and Others Focused—their teams feel no need to defend themselves and can focus on achieving goals without the fear of failing. This brings out the very best in teams and team members individually."

Recall now that Vanessa's findings were based on a little over 20,000 data points. (That's more than enough to provide statistically valid conclusions.) I asked David how many data points Human Synergistics had to support its findings. His answer: over two million.[12] On top of that, Human Synergistics had enough data to produce what's called a "normative group." This group of 14,000 leaders, which yielded more than 112,000 data points, was selected specifically for its ability to represent a large variety of demographic possibilities—men, women, old, young, from various countries around the world, in a variety of industries, and across the gamut of levels of leadership. Human Synergistics's normative group data confirmed that no matter the demographic split, the story is the same: How well-developed we are as people is the most significant determiner of how effective we will be as leaders.

CULTURAL NEUTRALITY

A few months after meeting with David for the first time, I had the opportunity to personally witness the cultural neutrality of *Who* Not What*. I was in Malaysia with the leaders of the $1 billion (USD) joint venture of my client. In the room were 50 leaders of business units in various countries throughout Asia and the Middle East. I asked them, as I do many groups I address, to describe the best leaders they've ever followed. Their answers were no different than what I had heard previously in North America and Australia. They described leaders who were Inwardly Sound and Others Focused. Their descriptions mirrored what Human Synergistics' normative group had already proven. As the CEO of that joint venture said,

> *"I have shared the concept [of Who* Not What] with many people in Asia: they get it right away."*

There is nothing culturally biased about *Who* Not What*. It is simply a truth about leadership and humanity.

The data Vanessa had analyzed, though scientifically verifiable on its own, was not on its own at all. Human Synergistics had multiple decades and millions of data points across numerous cultures and levels of leadership that supported it. KRW had hard financial evidence for it. The verdict was—and is—in: *Who* Not What* is a statistically verifiable reality.

I ASKED DAVID HOW MANY DATA POINTS HUMAN SYNERGISTICS HAD TO SUPPORT ITS FINDINGS. HIS ANSWER: OVER TWO MILLION.

Given all this evidence, you might think that when people first encounter this data they would immediately begin restructuring their own leadership development efforts and that of their organizations to take the simple truth of *Who* Not What* into account. But often they don't. There's a hesitation. And though I might want to be frustrated with that hesitation, I must remember my own reaction when I was first confronted with the statistical facts about *Who**

Not What. Though I was enthralled by what the data said, I didn't fully grasp its significance . . . not at first, anyway. I characterized the dominant two leadership categories of Inwardly Sound and Others Focused just as others in our consulting firm did, as mere behaviors and skills of leadership.

It wasn't until years later, in the quiet of my office one afternoon, that the differences between what leaders do and who they are hit me. And it took another five years after that for me to thoroughly grasp the connection between the two. Understanding both the differences and connections between the *Who* and *What* of leadership is essential if we are to put the truth of *Who** *Not What* to work. So that is where we will turn our attention next.

"The way of paradoxes is the way of truth."
OSCAR WILDE

CHAPTER FOUR

Chasm and Connection

UNDERSTANDING THE RELATIONSHIP BETWEEN
THE *WHO* AND *WHAT* OF LEADERSHIP

So far we've been learning what *Who* Not What* is and testing it to see if it's real and true. We've approached it with our gut-level intuition, the heartfelt emotions of our personal experiences, and our intellectual minds with research data. But any one of these could deceive us in a given moment. While it's comforting to say, "Always trust your gut," an objective analysis of decision-making would show that our gut-level intuition isn't always correct. You don't need a PhD to know that the emotions in our hearts can blind us to reality. And when it comes to head knowledge and data, statistics really can be manipulated to support a preconceived belief.

But what should we conclude when our guts, hearts, and minds all point in the same direction? What are the chances all three could be wrong at the same time? I'd argue that if we encounter an idea that is simultaneously supported by intuition, emotion, and intellect, we've encountered something that is real. We've encountered truth. *Who* Not What* is real. *Who* Not What* is true.

That said, there's still a lot of work to do if we want to leverage this truth for ourselves as leaders, for the organizations we lead, for the people who follow us, or to help us determine which leaders in our own lives are worth following. The next step is to more fully explore and understand the crucial differences and connections between the *Who* and *What* of leadership. To do that, we need to briefly go back to the story I shared in the Introduction.

So there I was that day in Atlanta, staring at the "behaviors and skills of leadership" on my whiteboard. It occurred to me that there was something different about the leadership categories of Inwardly Sound and Others Focused.[1] These two weren't different just because I knew the statistics about them. They were different by nature from the other components of leadership. The concepts that lived within Inwardly Sound and Others Focused could double as a list of the best qualities a person can have. They described who leaders are as people as opposed to what they do.

That difference may sound subtle and insignificant, but it's not. Let me illustrate with a story based on a real-life event.[2]

OPPORTUNITY KNOCKS

Greg was an up-and-coming leader at Perfect Paper, a paper manufacturer based in Tampa, Florida. At 32, Greg had just been promoted to General Manager of the company's Wichita, Kansas, manufacturing facility. His promotion to the role was simple. His boss, Marcus, was retiring, and no one else in the building had Greg's intellectual capacity and business acumen. Greg had proven himself by leading and completing many cost saving and efficiency improvement projects. Through these projects, he'd added millions of dollars to the company's bottom line over the years.

Marcus once said, "If you ask Greg to figure out how to make a process better, you can count him to do it, plain and simple. He's not the kind of guy who sells snow to Eskimos. He calculates why Eskimos should buy snow and then shows them the numbers."

With Greg as a shoo-in for the promotion, Marcus's exit interview was mostly a series of detailed questions about working with Greg. One potential concern that came up was Greg's interactions with his co-workers.

THE CONCEPTS THAT LIVED WITHIN INWARDLY SOUND AND OTHERS FOCUSED COULD DOUBLE AS A LIST OF THE BEST QUALITIES A PERSON CAN HAVE.

"Yes," Marcus said, "in the midst of Greg's process improvement projects, he did have moments when he rubbed our line employees the wrong way. I don't think he did it intentionally, but he drove so hard for results at times that it got the kind of attention he shouldn't want. I smoothed things over with the staff and asked Greg to be a little more careful in how he approached the team. He agreed, but was nonchalant about it. It's probably something to keep an eye on. But hey, no one's perfect. And this guy understands the business inside and out. He'll do a bang-up job as GM."

The first few months of Greg's tenure as GM were uneventful. Production rates and quality were steady. No major hiring

*3/4 OF YOUR EFFECTIVENESS AS A LEADER COMES FROM WHO YOU ARE, NOT WHAT YOU DO

or firing issues arose. It was a good time for him to ease into his new responsibilities. But after four months, Greg was summoned to company headquarters in Tampa. When he arrived, he found a room full of his peers—other GMs from the company's 12 production facilities around the country. There was tension in the air.

TARGETED FROM ABROAD

Larry was the President and CEO of Perfect Paper. He was a 34-year veteran of the company and had been in his current role for 10 years. He was moderately liked. Over the previous decade, he had guided the company to maintain its competitiveness in spite of increasing cost pressures.

> "WE HAVE A BIG CHALLENGE IN FRONT OF US. EVERYONE WILL HAVE TO PITCH IN IF WE'RE TO SURVIVE AS A COMPANY."
> — LARRY, CEO OF PERFECT PAPER

"Ladies and gentlemen, I won't sugarcoat things," Larry said. "We have a big challenge in front of us. Everyone will have to pitch in if we're to survive as a company."

The room looked stunned. What could have possibly created such a dire situation?

Larry explained that a Chinese competitor had targeted not one but all of Perfect Paper's clients. It appeared that the competitor was flush with cash and willing to undercut Perfect Paper's prices—even selling at a loss over a long period of time—to eliminate Perfect Paper as a competitor and company.

"Why us?" was the general sentiment around the room. There was no answer to that question.

"Folks," Larry said, "we *have* to figure out a way to cut 3.2% of our production costs across the board. By getting as lean as possible and dropping our prices, we might be able convince our Chinese 'friends' to target another company. Let me be clear: this isn't a momentary belt-tightening. It may take five years to make this go away. Our modifications can't be temporary."

The GMs left Tampa to return to their facilities with a mix of shock, fear, and determination. Greg immediately called an all-hands-on-deck meeting in Wichita. He told everyone they could expect major changes and that ongoing employment couldn't be promised, not even to employees who participated fully in cost-reduction efforts. The entire meeting took about 10 minutes. Everyone was shaken.

Over the next six months, Greg and his team reduced production costs by 1.1%. He was proud of the effort, but he also realized it fell short of the need. The stress built inside him bit by bit each day.

AN UNEXPECTED CALL

One Saturday morning, Greg got a call from Bob, head of HR in Tampa. Saturday phone calls weren't the norm for Perfect Paper, even under the current circumstances.

Greg thought something was up. He was right.

"Greg, I'm calling you at home over the weekend on purpose," Bob said. "I wanted to give you time to digest what I have to say."

Greg felt a twinge in his stomach.

"We received a letter signed by 27 workers in your facility," Bob said. "They say working for you is unpleasant. They say you've been riding them hard. They claim you speak harshly to

---

*3/4 OF YOUR EFFECTIVENESS AS A LEADER COMES FROM WHO YOU ARE, NOT WHAT YOU DO

them. They sound hurt and upset."

"Come on, Bob," Greg said. "Times are tough. They're overreacting. We're at 1.1% of our 3.2% cost reduction goal. They know we need to do better. They're just scared and lashing out. They need someone to blame, and they're biting the hand that feeds them. Yes, I'm pushing them, but how else can we survive?"

"Well, Greg," Bob said, "we think it's a bigger deal than that. I've talked about it with Larry and we're in agreement. We're going to send you off-site for a week of communication training. We have your plane ticket. You leave first thing Monday morning."

Bob continued, "I know news like this isn't easy to hear, but this can be a big positive for you. We still believe in you or we wouldn't make this investment. The program costs $18,000 (USD) for the week. I don't share that with you to put pressure on you, only to let you know that we believe in making that investment in you."

"Thanks, Bob. I appreciate it. I'll keep that in mind."

Greg hung up. He was angry and a little confused. *Why didn't our folks come and talk to me directly?* he wondered.

PICKING UP NEW SKILLS

Greg's journey to the *Communicate How? Communicate Now!* program in Poughkeepsie, New York, began with an early Monday morning flight. It felt strange to be on a plane heading far away on what should've been a normal Monday morning at the plant. At 33,000 feet, Greg readied himself for what he was sure would feel like a long week.

But, instead, the week flew by. Greg learned a number of

simple, practical strategies that made sense: nod your head when listening to others, repeat back to people what you've heard them say, affirm their perspectives even when you don't agree with them, and, above all, don't interrupt others (to which Greg mentally added, *Even when what they are saying is stupid*).

As the final session of the week came to a close, Greg was looking forward to returning to Wichita to try out his new communication techniques. He was surprised to see a number of his *Communicate How? Communicate Now!* colleagues hugging each other and exchanging contact information at the course's end. *What was the point of that? It was only a week-long conference, and they'll never see each other again,* Greg thought to himself.

As he walked into the manufacturing facility early the following Monday morning, Greg felt strangely comfortable. His hope for what could be improved outweighed his concern for seeing his employees for the first time since they'd sent that letter to corporate. He considered

GREG CONSIDERED LETTING THE WHOLE TEAM KNOW WHERE HE'D BEEN, BUT HE DIDN'T WANT TO INTERRUPT THE PRODUCTION SCHEDULE FOR THE MORNING.

letting the whole team know where he'd been, but he didn't want to interrupt the production schedule for the morning. He decided it was best to put what he'd learned to use and let his actions speak for themselves.

Six months passed. Cost reduction improved to 1.7%—still short of the 3.2% goal. Progress was too slow. Greg's stress was building. *We're starting to live on borrowed time,* he thought.

---

*3/4 OF YOUR EFFECTIVENESS AS A LEADER COMES FROM WHO YOU ARE, NOT WHAT YOU DO

Then came another Saturday-morning phone call.

BACKCHANNEL AND BACKSLIDE

"Greg, it's Bob in Tampa."

Greg began to sweat. Maybe it was good news. He tried to calm his racing pulse back to normal.

"How are things going?" Bob asked.

"We're still a long way off from our cost reduction goal of 3.2%," Greg said. "I think it's weighing heavily on everyone."

"I'm sure it is," Bob said. "What about your interactions with your staff?"

"As well as can be expected under these stressful circumstances."

"How would you evaluate your communication with the team? How well have you been applying what you learned in Poughkeepsie?"

"Pretty well, I think," Greg said. "I was gangbusters when I returned, pausing every day to think about how I was communicating. I applied the techniques I learned in almost every meeting."

"That's the feedback I received as well," Bob said. "When we get complaints of the sort we received about you, we set up an open communication channel between corporate and those in the field. We didn't tell you about it because we didn't want to skew the results or create additional discomfort between you and your employees. Through that channel, your employees said you behaved differently when you returned from Poughkeepsie. You were a much more effective communicator. But I'm afraid that improvement hasn't held up," Bob said.

"What do you mean?"

"Your employees say you've gradually returned to your old ways over the last six months, Greg. They even said the last 30 days have been worse than before we sent you to the off-site program."

"That's disappointing to hear," Greg said.

"I agree," said Bob.

"I want to ask you a question, Bob. I probably should've asked you this before I went to communication training. Why does the way my employees feel matter so much? I have two kids, two and four years old. I love them to death, but if I operated out of how they were feeling all the time, they'd never go to bed and would eat nothing but ice cream all day long. So why does it matter so much how people feel? Shouldn't it matter more whether we're hitting our numbers?"

"Greg, if we don't hit our numbers, we won't survive. So, yes, numbers matter a lot. But it sounds as though you think the employees at the plant don't really matter as individuals— that their only real utility is in the dollars they produce for the company. Is that right?"

"When you put it that way, it doesn't sound good," Greg said. "But we aren't here to make each other happy. We're here to make money for the company. The company pays us to do so. It's a simple exchange. That perspective has served me well. Earlier in my career here, it helped me complete cost saving projects. And eventually, it got me promoted to GM."

Bob replied, "We didn't do a proper job of vetting you for a leadership role of this magnitude, Greg. Things are worse than you realize. Even in this tough economy, you have a significant number of employees ready to quit, including your Assistant GM. We can't keep you in your current role any longer. Because we dropped the ball in the vetting process, we're going to give you two options. We have a generous severance offer for you or, if you'd like to stay with us, we have an Assistant GM position in Toledo, Ohio, where you could have a fresh start. We're open to either, but we can't go on with things as they've been. I'm sorry."

Greg's blood was boiling. "I'd rather be fired for not achieving the 3.2% cost reduction over the last 12 months than for not coddling the people who work here. No one coddled me over the last 10 years."

"Marcus did a lot over the years to take you into account as an individual," Bob said.

Greg was so angry he was barely listening. "I'm not interested in a fresh start inside this company," he said. "Let's talk about the severance package."

DEEPER THAN BEHAVIOR

As you read this story, what did you think was Greg's biggest leadership challenge? His employees' number-one complaint was his poor communication, but communication wasn't really the issue. The techniques Greg learned in Poughkeepsie didn't stick because of who Greg was as a person. His perspectives on life and work caused him to objectify people. His empathy and emotional intelligence were under-developed. Down deep, at least in the workplace, Greg didn't value people beyond how much paper they could manufacture. He viewed employees like children rather than adults and peers. He judged them for being hurt by his words.

Greg's leadership failure wasn't about what he did. It was about who he was. His communication training didn't produce long-term value because it only treated the symptom: Greg's actions. It didn't affect Greg as a person.

The reaction of Perfect Paper's corporate leaders is important in this story as well. Bob and Larry agreed that sending Greg to communication training was the right move. This is a typical organizational reaction to problems such as Greg's. Bob and Larry threw behavior modification at an issue that actually went much deeper than mere behavior. This is the leadership development equivalent of bringing a knife to a gunfight. In the end, the company wasted a week of Greg's time, $18,000 (USD),

THE TRAINING DIDN'T PRODUCE LONG-TERM VALUE BECAUSE IT ONLY TREATED THE SYMPTOM: GREG'S ACTIONS. IT DIDN'T AFFECT GREG AS A PERSON.

and six months of hoping for a better result. Disgruntled employees had to live with a problematic leader for an additional six months after the training.

Even the company that hosted the communication training program paid a price. No doubt their reputation suffered within the walls of Perfect Paper. They became known as an expensive option that doesn't produce results. All of this damage, inefficiency, disappointment, and waste existed because Perfect Paper's corporate leaders didn't understand the difference between the *Who* and *What* of Greg's leadership. Maybe Greg could have developed enough to effectively take on the role of GM, but we'll never know for sure. His development as a leader was aimed at *What* when it should've been aimed at *Who*.

*3/4 OF YOUR EFFECTIVENESS AS A LEADER COMES FROM WHO YOU ARE, NOT WHAT YOU DO

THE BLESSING OF ISABELLA

The difference between the *Who* and *What* of leadership is not only on display in leadership failures. It can also be seen in leadership successes. There are times when being a well-developed *Who* overcomes gaps in the *What* of leadership. Such was the case with Isabella.

Isabella grew up on a farm about 30 minutes outside of Erie, Pennsylvania. She loved kids and was interested in dentistry. In college she studied pre-dental. In time, she became a doctor of both pediatric dentistry and orthodontics. She went on to work simultaneously as a pediatric dentist and a dental school professor.

Over time, Isabella noticed that there were limited orthodontics services available in the greater-Erie area. So she began seeing orthodontics patients in the evenings at a local doctor's office. The vast majority of these patients were children whom she saw at their parents' request. As demand grew, she rented daytime space from a local nursing home. And in one short season, not wanting to interrupt her patients' brace-tightening schedules by yet another office move, she set up a dental chair in her home and treated patients there.

After five years of being in orthodontics "on the side," Isabella left the security of her pediatric dentistry and dental school professor roles to treat orthodontics patients full time. The next five years saw continued expansion in the business. After a decade of success, Isabella felt blessed—so much so that she and her husband decided to shut the business down for an entire week and take all of its employees on a cruise. After 18 years of being in business, Isabella found herself owning a company with 23 full-time employees and $4 million (USD) in annual revenue.

At that time, both a regional orthodontics practice and a national dental care provider came calling. Each wanted to buy the business from Isabella. The offer from the national dental care provider was far more lucrative, but Isabella turned it down. Instead, she sold the lion's share of the business to the regional orthodontics practice while maintaining a small portion of ownership for herself. The regional orthodontics practice recognized that one of the business's greatest assets was Isabella herself and asked her to stay on as president. She agreed, and that's what Isabella did for 22 years until her retirement.

HIDDEN SOURCE

You might assume that Isabella's success came through a combination of business knowledge and orthodontics expertise. But that's not true. While Isabella was an exceptional clinician with national recognition for her orthodontics work, she had no formal education in business at all. She learned everything she knew about business from the school of hard knocks.

If you want to know the key to Isabella's business success, consider the woman who treated orthodontics patients in her home. Isabella loves helping people. She's renowned for treating more than their dental ailments—so much so that she has a book in her den full of notes from patients, parents, and students about the impact she's had on their lives.

I've known Isabella for many years. She's as Others Focused as any leader I've ever met. Her inner core—who she is—helped her leverage her orthodontics knowledge into a business that today has a 17,000-square-foot flagship facility, numerous satellite offices, more than 70 full-time employees, and more than $11 million (USD) in annual revenues.

*3/4 OF YOUR EFFECTIVENESS AS A LEADER COMES FROM WHO YOU ARE, NOT WHAT YOU DO

Isabella wanted to help people. That defined the way she interacted with students, patients, her patients' parents . . . and her employees. Her concern for others produced loyalty in her employees. Isabella is a caring woman of great wisdom and generosity. That's why people have followed her. That's why they've given the above-and-beyond efforts that have enabled Isabella to build her business without a formal business education. *Who* has the power to overcome gaps in *What.*

A few years ago, I was in Isabella's office when I stumbled upon a Boss's Day card. The handwritten note on the inside of the card said, "Isabella, I can't thank you enough for the blessed privilege of working for you. Thank you for helping me to grow the past eight years . . . physically, mentally, spiritually, and emotionally! God bless you always! — Gwen"

It wasn't a well-crafted businesses strategy or a specific leadership skill that inspired Gwen to write that note. Isabella inspired it—who she is as a person inspired it. How engaged would you guess Gwen was in her job? Do you think she'd leave the company for a small bump in pay? Her engagement and loyalty are tangible business advantages. Isabella may not have been who she was in order to gain those strategic business advantages, but she got them nonetheless. Engagement and loyalty are rarely products of the *What* of leadership. These business advantages are the spoils of being a leader who is a well-developed *Who*—a leader worth following.

THE CHASM

The difference between a leader's actions and who he or she is as a person might seem indistinguishable at first. After all, one can legitimately argue that our actions are a reflection of who we are.

But it's not quite that simple.

It's possible for us to "go through the motions" and live out actions that don't completely align with who we are. As leaders, when our actions aren't wholeheartedly pouring out of who we are as people, they're incomplete. In those instances, our efforts lack the depth and sincerity that make them most valuable to those around us. Understanding the distinction between the *Who* and *What* of leadership helps us understand the lack of impact some leaders have even when they seem to be making the right decisions.

ENGAGEMENT AND LOYALTY ARE RARELY PRODUCTS OF THE *WHAT* OF LEADERSHIP.

Another advantage in seeing the crucial difference between the *Who* and *What* of leadership comes in finding effective solutions. We can't solve *Who* problems with *What* solutions (and vice versa). Just look back at Greg's story earlier in this chapter. Greg's leaders, Bob and Larry, attempted to solve a *Who* problem with a *What* solution. Not surprisingly, it was a fantastic failure.

The existence of a chasm between the *Who* and *What* of leadership is not the end of the story, however. Despite their differences, there is a deep connection between *Who* and *What*. The chasm and connection coexist. To show how this works, let's look at one of the most common objects on planet Earth: the tree.

BELOW GROUND

I love trees. I have pictures of them all over my office. They remind me why I do what I do. A tree is the perfect representation of a leader. Though each tree has the same parts, each is unique. The environments in which they live can have an enormous influ-

*3/4 OF YOUR EFFECTIVENESS AS A LEADER COMES FROM WHO YOU ARE, NOT WHAT YOU DO

ence on how weak or strong they become. Trees can be planted and nourished intentionally, yet some grow strong without the benefit of such care. They can get sick and recover. They can get sick and die. And none are strong and healthy without a well-developed root system.

If you were to use the tree as a metaphor for the leader, knowing what you know now about the *Who* Not What Principle,* what parts of the tree would represent Inwardly Sound and Others Focused? That's right, the roots.

Just as a tree is dependent on its roots for health and growth, so too is the effectiveness of *what the leader does* dependent on *who the leader is* as a person. Just as it is impossible for the tree to reach its potential without healthy roots, it is impossible for leaders to reach their full potential without being Inwardly Sound and Others Focused.

THE CONNECTION

"But why?" you may ask. "What's the relationship between the *Who* and *What?*"

Who makes the *What* matter. That is the enduring and profound connection between them.

While intellect, competency, and experience are factors, the lion's share of a leader's credibility comes from who the leader is as a person. We listen more intently, get on board more readily, and work more enthusiastically for leaders who are Inwardly Sound and Others Focused. Everything we hear and see from them is colored by our understanding of who they are. Like it or not, admit to it or not, be consciously aware of it or not, we hear the words from the mouths of well-developed people differently than from those who are not well developed. When leaders step

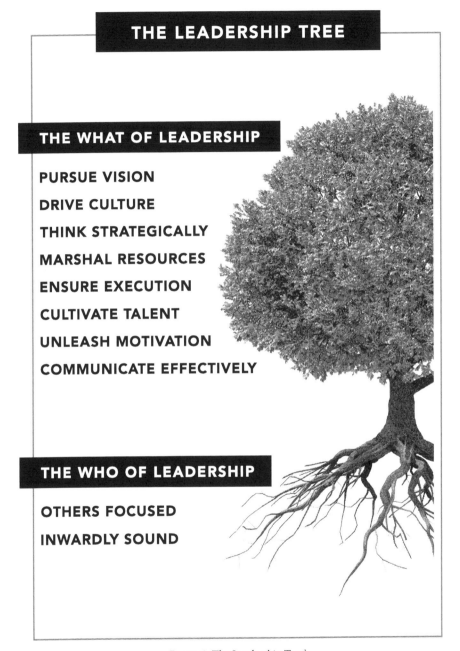

THE LEADERSHIP TREE

THE WHAT OF LEADERSHIP

PURSUE VISION

DRIVE CULTURE

THINK STRATEGICALLY

MARSHAL RESOURCES

ENSURE EXECUTION

CULTIVATE TALENT

UNLEASH MOTIVATION

COMMUNICATE EFFECTIVELY

THE WHO OF LEADERSHIP

OTHERS FOCUSED

INWARDLY SOUND

Figure 6: The Leadership Tree[3]

*3/4 OF YOUR EFFECTIVENESS AS A LEADER COMES FROM WHO YOU ARE, NOT WHAT YOU DO

to the front of the room, who they are determines whether we're fully on board with them or reluctantly giving the minimum that the job requires. Who our leaders are as people—well developed or not—is the primary factor in whether they get the "want to" or only the "have to" of our efforts.

Over the years, I've hosted many conversations about the aspects of leadership listed in The Leadership Tree (Figure 6 on page 57). One common conversation is about the need for leaders to motivate and inspire their followers. I'll ask a group of people to discuss the difference between motivation, inspiration, and manipulation. The general consensus is that manipulation involves a leader getting people to do what the leader wants for the leader's own purposes.[4] Next comes a debate about the internal and external natures of motivation and inspiration.

Eventually, when those in the room talk about what drives them to greater heights as followers, what touches them deeply and inspires them is the essence of the leader they're following. Is the leader someone who stands for and values something bigger than themselves? Is the leader noble? Is the leader someone worth following? This is what inspires followers.

It's hard to miss the connection between who the leader is as a person and what inspires followers. This is just a single example of how *Who* makes *What* matter.

We can look at the content in each part of the *What* of leadership and see its direct connection to *Who*. Even Think Strategically, the *What* category that appears most dissociated from Inwardly Sound and Others Focused, has a solid connection. Humble (from Others Focused) leaders tend to ask more questions, take more input, and be more open to others' perspectives. Secure and settled (from Inwardly Sound) leaders feel less threatened than leaders who are not secure and settled. They're more willing to have the smartest people in the room participate in decision-making. The combination of humility, personal security, and inner settledness significantly improves the quality of the inputs a leader uses to understand and make strategic decisions. As the quality of the inputs determines the quality of outputs, even strategic thinking is influenced by the degree to which a leader is Inwardly Sound and Others Focused.

WHICH COMES FIRST?

I'd like to take a moment to point to the order in which you see Inwardly Sound and Others Focused in The Leadership Tree. Notice that Inwardly Sound sits below being Others Focused. That's intentional. It's difficult, if not impossible, to give out of what we don't have.

If a leader attempts to become Others Focused without being Inwardly Sound, it's like trying to get blood out of a turnip . . . or perhaps, more accurately in this case, blood out of a not-fully-developed turnip. It's understandable and perhaps even noble that leaders would become exclusively focused on being more Others Focused upon learning about *Who* Not What*. But don't make that mistake. Don't neglect becoming an Inwardly Sound leader. It will catch up to you. The aspects of being Inwardly Sound are not only essential components for becoming a well-developed *Who*, they also enable you to become Others Focused in a healthy, sustainable way.

SIMULTANEOUSLY

So that's the full picture of the relationship between the *Who* and *What* of leadership. A simple tree tells the story. While the roots

---

*3/4 OF YOUR EFFECTIVENESS AS A LEADER COMES FROM WHO YOU ARE, NOT WHAT YOU DO

are uniquely different than the rest of the tree, they could not possibly be more influential in determining the prosperity of the tree. The chasm and connection between the *Who* and *What* of leadership exist simultaneously.

The Leadership Tree metaphor has invited me to notice the trees around me more than I otherwise would have. I hope the same for you. Maybe the next time you see a particularly impressive tree, you'll think of all the time and effort that went into its growth . . . and of the hidden roots that enable it to thrive.

Now that we're armed with this understanding, we're going to take an in-depth look at the roots of the tree. What lives within them that makes them so valuable to leaders and, subsequently, their followers? It's time to unearth the answer to that question. Grab your shovel. Let's dig in.

*"The process of becoming a leader is similar,
if not identical, to becoming a fully integrated human being."*
WARREN BENNIS

CHAPTER FIVE

Defining What It Means To Be Inwardly Sound

THE WELL-DEVELOPED *WHO*: PART ONE

It isn't all that useful to say, "If you want to reach your potential as a leader, you must become the best *Who* you can be. Thank you, and good night." We need more if we're going to put the truth of *Who* * *Not* *What* to work for us and for those we lead.

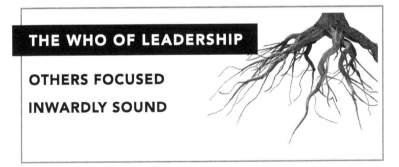

THE WHO OF LEADERSHIP

OTHERS FOCUSED

INWARDLY SOUND

Figure 7: The Who of Leadership

In this and the following two chapters, we will explore in detail what it means to be a well-developed *Who*—Inwardly Sound and Others Focused[1]—not merely by action but by thinking, belief, and perspective. Take care not to be fooled by the seemingly familiar words you will read. Some leaders are tempted to skim the topics covered, nod in simple, unexplored agreement, and even assume they've got 80% or 90% of each one figured out. A more thoughtful investigation will yield a far more valuable result for you.

In my work with executive teams, we typically spend three to four months on each of the aspects of Inwardly Sound and Others Focused. We call these "journeys" because that is exactly what they are: intensive and in-depth expeditions of self-discovery.

Why spend three to four months on concepts that many people quickly agree with? No one has ever gotten physically healthier by agreeing with a textbook about working out. Similarly, it isn't the understanding of these ideas that makes us more well-developed *Whos* and more effective leaders. Rather, it is concentrated effort applied in everyday leadership moments over time that enables leaders to grow. It is the refining fire of real-life application seen through the lens of the *Who* Not What Principle* that brings true development.

This journey is not about quick wins or short-term gains. What is asked of leaders who wish to become their very best is far deeper and more demanding than mere tips, tricks, and tactics. When done effectively, this journey is surgery simultaneously performed on both the brain and the heart.

My hope in communicating the challenging reality of this journey is to encourage you to have an explorer's mentality. It is a perspective that is hopeful, curious, and open. And it will cause you to feel the anxiety and excitement that every explorer experiences when they are about to set out. What will you find out about yourself? Will you discover you are better or worse than you thought? Will you find that you have been wise or unwise in how you have selected leaders to follow in your past? What will you do about what you discover? Will you succeed in your desire to identify leaders who are worth following? If it is your mission to do so, will you succeed in becoming a leader worth following? These are scary and wonderful questions that I invite you to bravely engage with as we unpack in detail what it means to be Inwardly Sound and Others Focused.

With that said, let's begin by investigating what it means to be Inwardly Sound.

INWARDLY SOUND

On November 29, 1993, Mr. Kim MacCartney, a marine surveyor for the Insurance Company of North America, inspected the *El Toro II,* a rockfishing boat working in the Chesapeake Bay. MacCartney found numerous safety problems but saw nothing to suggest the hull wasn't seaworthy. "Structurally, she looked in pretty good condition," he said.

Five days later, the *El Toro II* left on what proved to be its last voyage. In a storm roughly five miles from the coast of Point Lookout, Maryland, the hull of the boat ruptured. The Coast Guard responded to a mayday call but not before all 23 people on the ship had fallen into the dangerously cold waters. All suffered hypothermia. Three lost their lives due to exposure to the elements.

In the end, authorities determined that three loose planks in the hull were the culprits in the boat's sinking. Ensuing debates about who was to blame for not keeping the ship docked—the ship's owner, the insurance company inspector, or the Coast Guard—didn't change the fact that the boat sank because it was not a sound vessel.

*3/4 OF YOUR EFFECTIVENESS AS A LEADER COMES FROM WHO YOU ARE, NOT WHAT YOU DO

A truly sound vessel not only looks safe, it *is* safe. It can be counted on. It's stable even in rough waters. It doesn't crack under stress. It has structural integrity. It is trustworthy.

Now let me rewrite that last paragraph.

Inwardly Sound leaders not only look safe, they *are* safe. They can be counted on. They're stable even in rough waters. They don't crack under stress. They have structural integrity. They are trustworthy.

> **INWARDLY SOUND LEADERS NOT ONLY LOOK SAFE, THEY *ARE* SAFE. THEY CAN BE COUNTED ON.**

Does this sound like the type of leader you want to follow? Of course it does. Have you seen leaders that don't fit this description? Of course you have. Perhaps more importantly, does this sound like the type of leader you want to be? How could it not? Does this sound like the type of leader you've been? I'll leave that for you to answer.

If we were to map a path toward becoming Inwardly Sound, it would have six components, each of which has complexities and challenges worth investigating. For reasons that will become clear later, we're going to save one of those components to address in Chapter 7. In this chapter, we will address five aspects of being Inwardly Sound. Listed in order of importance, starting with the most crucial, they are:

Secure + Settled

Self-Aware

Principled

Holistically Healthy

Purposeful

SECURE + SETTLED

COMFORTABLE IN MY OWN SKIN
AND AT PEACE ABOUT WHAT
THE FUTURE MAY BRING

There is nothing more valuable to the inner health of leaders than being personally secure (as opposed to insecure) and settled. At a basic level, being secure and settled is the leader's ability to accurately answer, "Who am I?" "To whom do I matter?" and "Why do I matter?" while fully and peacefully accepting the answers to these questions. That may sound simple until you consider that, in order to be completely accurate, the answers to these questions must take into account one's failings and limitations.

I'M OK, AND COME WHAT MAY, I'M OK

Secure and settled leaders live comfortably in their own skin. A healthy portion of their self-worth is driven from within. Though they may enjoy, deserve, and receive accolades from those around them, they do not require a constant flow of praise to believe they are capable and valuable in the world. When the going becomes rough, they have perspectives and belief systems about themselves and life that anchor them. As a result, they are capable of providing safe harbor for those they lead, even in the midst of turmoil.

Leaders who are secure accept themselves for who they are, flaws and all. They invite others to do the same, but they don't need others to accept them in order to accept themselves. This is not to imply that they aren't motivated to grow and develop as people. Rather, they recognize their limitations and shortcomings even as they work to grow and develop as people.

Settled leaders have an inner stabilizer. Because of this, they lead with confidence despite their external circumstances—even circumstances that tempt them to question who they are and their ability to lead.

My colleague and friend John Ott summarizes it this way: "Secure leaders say, 'I'm OK.' Settled leaders say, 'Come what may, I'm OK.'"

INSECURE AND UNSETTLED

Insecure leaders, on the other hand, struggle to come to a place of rest about who they are. When unaddressed, they spend their lives spinning in an endless need for validation and reassurance. As a result, they unconsciously look to their followers to confirm their personal worth and value. This puts their followers in an awkward position that often leads to strained relationships, confused priorities, distraction from goals, and suboptimal performance.

Unsettled leaders live and lead out of a fear of the negatives that could befall them. They fear losses of income, status, power, and the like. Even if not expressed to others, they are consistently concerned about how events and other people might impact them. They model for those around them—most especially their subordinates—a spirit of self-preservation that limits their perspectives, the quality of their relationships, and their ability to focus on the greater good of others and the organization.

Catering to the inner maladies of these underdeveloped leaders often trumps healthy communication and a focus on the organization's needs. Consciously or unconsciously, making decisions and executing strategies that help these leaders feel more secure and settled becomes the task of those who follow insecure and unsettled leaders.

IS IT ACTUALLY ABOUT ME?

One of the greatest privileges of the work I do with leadership teams is getting to be a witness to how *Who* Not What* lands at home. When working with executives on being and becoming more secure and settled, I ask them to interview someone who is particularly secure and settled. One leader I worked with deftly chose to interview his children.

> **"SECURE LEADERS SAY, 'I'M OK.' SETTLED LEADERS SAY, 'COME WHAT MAY, I'M OK.'"**
> **— JOHN OTT**

In the midst of the interview, this executive/parent made an observation that brings home the significance of being secure and settled, not only for himself, but also for his kids. He said,

> *"When I did the interview with my kids, I realized that as parents we try to steer them toward a norm which, in fact, might create and cause insecurities they may not have had otherwise."*

That's a fascinating and insightful observation. It raises the questions: If I am pushing my kids, employees, and/or next generation of leaders in a particular direction, why am I doing it? Is it really for their own good and development, or is it to protect my ego or sense of self because they reflect on me? And if my intent is to develop secure and settled leaders, am I doing anything that could undermine that? In this, the connection between being secure and settled and how we cultivate the capabilities, perspectives, and heart of those we lead is palpable.

**3/4 OF YOUR EFFECTIVENESS AS A LEADER COMES FROM WHO YOU ARE, NOT WHAT YOU DO

FIGHT FOR IT

While the leadership benefits of becoming secure and settled are sizable, few proactively travel the path to get there. Why? Simply put, it's hard. Most leaders would rather put their heads down and work 20 hours a day than do the sticky work of wrestling with the inner questions of personal identity.

Success in this arena can be difficult to define, and issues rarely resolve quickly or are wrapped in a neat bow. But the payoff is worth it. Secure and settled leaders avoid twisted priorities and relational turmoil. Consistent relational and organizational efficiency are their rewards.

Expectation management

UNHEALTHY LEADERS WITH AN UNDERDEVELOPED SENSE OF IDENTITY UNCONSCIOUSLY LOOK TO THEIR FOLLOWERS TO VALIDATE THEIR PERSONAL WORTH AND VALUE. THIS CREATES AN UNHEALTHY DYNAMIC BETWEEN LEADER AND FOLLOWER.

tells us that when we know a battle will be difficult, we're able to stick it out longer. If that's true, poet E.E. Cummings's words are encouraging to leaders willing to travel the road to being secure and settled:

> "To be nobody-but-yourself—in a world which is doing its best, night and day, to make you everybody else— means to fight the hardest battle which any human being can fight; and never stop fighting."

To one extent or another, we all have identity issues that challenge our ability to be secure and settled. Being aware of and addressing those issues is a non-negotiable for leaders who want to reach their full potential.

SELF–AWARE

AN ACCURATE AND REASONABLE UNDERSTANDING OF WHO I AM—MY STRENGTHS, WEAKNESSES, QUIRKS, PREFERENCES, HOT BUTTONS, PERSONALITY STYLE, DENTS, AND WORLDVIEW—AND HOW WHO I AM AFFECTS OTHERS

Have you ever worked for a leader who lacked self-awareness? It was painful, wasn't it?

Self-awareness provides hope for every leader, not to mention hope for the people who follow that leader. A self-aware leader is capable of growing in areas of strength as well as deficiency. We can only improve what we know about, and self-aware leaders give themselves that opportunity. Understanding yourself as a person—strengths, weaknesses, quirks, preferences, hot buttons, personality style, dents, and worldview—is necessary in order to be intentional about how you lead your followers.

A lack of self-awareness, on the other hand, dooms leaders to personal stagnation. The path to improvement is limited for those who don't have their eyes open enough to see where they stand. And the negative consequences don't stop there. Followers who observe a lack of self-awareness in their leaders disconnect emotionally from those leaders. No one wants to follow an out-of-touch leader. Being out of touch with the reality of our own (especially negative) impact as leaders is one of the most egre-

*3/4 OF YOUR EFFECTIVENESS AS A LEADER COMES FROM WHO YOU ARE, NOT WHAT YOU DO

gious forms of leadership failure we can commit. This is what followers joke about at the water cooler when the leader isn't within earshot.

As if that weren't enough, leaders who aren't self-aware provide a bad example to their followers. Their followers have no one to emulate in becoming more self-aware. This shortcoming encourages followers to repeat the sins of their leaders. It truly becomes the blind leading the blind.

THE STATISTICS OF SELF-AWARENESS

The effects of self-awareness in leadership are seen not only in the logic of psychology and relationships, but also in the bottom line of financial performance. In a Korn Ferry International study of just under 7,000 leaders in more than 450 publicly traded companies, Dr. David Zes and Dr. Dana Landis found that the employees of companies with lower rates of return had 20% more leadership "blind spots" (i.e., lower self-awareness) than their counterparts in higher performing companies. Additionally, they found that employees in companies with lower financial performance were 79% more likely to have low overall self-awareness when compared to employees of companies with higher financial rates of return.[2]

Receiving the kind of tough-but-true feedback necessary to create greater self-awareness isn't easy. It can be especially difficult for leaders because so often there are organizational and cultural barriers to followers providing transparent and complete feedback to the people who lead them. Many times, plain old fear keeps followers from being honest about their experiences with a leader. Unfortunately, this makes the fully self-aware leader a rare animal.

Dr. Tasha Eurich, an organizational psychologist, reports that just 10% to 15% of leaders are self-aware.[3] The likelihood of the leader being self-aware decreases as power and influence increase. Says Eurich:

". . . the more power a leader holds, the more likely they are to overestimate their skills and abilities. One study of more than 3,600 leaders across a variety of roles and industries found that, relative to lower-level leaders, higher-level leaders more significantly overvalued their skills (compared with others' perceptions).[4] In fact, this pattern existed for 19 out of the 20 competencies the researchers measured, including emotional self-awareness, accurate self-assessment, empathy, trustworthiness, and leadership performance.

"Researchers have proposed two primary explanations for this phenomenon. First, by virtue of their level, senior leaders simply have fewer people above them who can provide candid feedback. Second, the more power a leader wields, the less comfortable people will be to give them constructive feedback, for fear it will hurt their careers. Business professor James O'Toole has added that, as one's power grows, one's willingness to listen shrinks, either because they think they know more than their employees or because seeking feedback will come at a cost." [5, 6]

Here we begin to see connections between different aspects of being Inwardly Sound. Mature, healthy, and well-developed views regarding one's personal identity go a long way toward lowering the barrier to candid feedback that the power dynamic between leaders and followers creates. Therefore, being secure and settled—which will be covered later in this chapter—helps open the door to greater self-awareness for leaders.

THE LEADERS WE'VE FOLLOWED

When I work with leaders on the issue of self-awareness, I invite them to recall their experiences in following leaders who were not self-aware. Such stories often provide motivation to do the tough work required to become and remain self-aware.

When asked about following leaders who are not self-aware, one client shared the following observation:

> ". . . on two occasions I have worked for leaders who were self-_unaware_ or perhaps just did not care how they impacted people. I found witnessing this very disturbing on two fronts. I did not like to witness these leaders hurting others and I felt extremely sorry for the leaders as I thought they might have suffered from something deeper emotionally . . . I do think they suffered from not building strong commitment with those around them. I saw a lot of people try to avoid or worse yet exit the organization because of these leaders' self-_unawareness_."

Whether self-aware or self-unaware, leaders will experience pain and difficulty. It will either be the pain and difficulty of pursuing and receiving challenging feedback, which can lead to accelerated personal growth and improved relationships, or it will be the pain and difficulty of the negative outcomes that show up when we don't create safe paths for transparent feedback from those we lead and influence.

Growing in self-awareness is not guaranteed for the leader. In fact, the deck is stacked against it. As leaders increase their stature, the barriers to transparent feedback increase as well. Only the most intentional, courageous, and humble of leaders will create for themselves the opportunity to become more self-aware as their influence grows—all in service of being and becoming a leader worth following.

PRINCIPLED

There's nothing complicated about this one. Leaders who pass the tests of being principled earn our trust. While there are many ways to articulate what it means to be principled, I encourage leaders to consider a definition with five aspects.

COURAGEOUS	**MOVE FORWARD IN THE FACE OF FEAR**
HONEST	**ASCERTAIN THE TRUTH CAREFULLY AND COMMUNICATE IT ACCURATELY**
AUTHENTIC	**GENUINELY SHARE HOW I THINK, WHAT I FEEL, AND WHO I AM**
INTEGRITY	**DO WHAT I SAY I WILL ... AND PROACTIVELY ADMIT WHEN I DON'T**
GRIT	**LEVERAGE MENTAL FORTITUDE TO PRODUCE COMMITMENT AND DETERMINATION**

Each of these qualities has unique depth. When fully investigated, they become more complex than what they first appear to be.

- When does courage cross over and become unwise risk-taking?

- Is it dishonest that not everyone gets all of the information available to the leader?

- Regarding authenticity, what is the difference between sharing what I think and sharing how I think?

- If I don't do what I say I will, but readily admit to it each time it happens, will I still have integrity?

- Is there such a thing as too much grit that actually gets leaders and their followers into trouble?

Despite the complexities that live within the five aspects of being principled, each directly connects to the trustworthiness of the leader. The functional, emotional, and relational value of trust in leadership cannot be underestimated. Everything the leader attempts to do is built on it. Thus understanding what it means to be principled and living that out is critical for all leaders who are serious about reaching their leadership potential.

Few people argue against the positive effect of being a principled leader, but rarely is it intentionally developed in the work environment. That's unfortunate for two reasons. First, when we get away from sensational headlines about shocking ethical breaches by high profile leaders that make morality look like simple black and white realities, we see that a great number of leadership's moral challenges show up in the gray—those areas subject to nuance and interpretation. This reality is a wide-open door to leadership development that too few leaders and organizations walk through.

Second, though some believe moral growth doesn't occur

outside of childhood and adolescence, research has shown that principles (ethics and morals) can be developed in adults. Researchers Cheryl Armon and Theo Dawson produced data that showed that moral development within people can increase until the end of their lives.[7] Their work supported similar theories by Harvard researcher Lawrence Kohlberg and University of Minnesota researcher James Rest.[8]

These two realities—the gray of the majority of moral temptations and the ability of adults to become more principled—become especially important to consider when combined with a psychological phenomenon called the Better-Than-Average (BTA) Effect. The BTA Effect is the human tendency to see ourselves as better than others. Studies have found that the BTA Effect is strongest in "important" attributes such as the character qualities that make someone principled.[9]

I've seen this up close and personal. I once took a poll in an organization asking people in leadership positions to rate the overall honesty of the people in their company, its leaders, and themselves. Even after concluding that the company and its leaders were significantly more honest than the general public, 154 out of 155 leaders surveyed concluded they were personally just as or more honest than their peers within the company.

We are naturally predisposed to see ourselves as better than we are. It's a mistake, therefore, for leaders to conclude that their self-assessed morality is totally accurate or that their moral development is complete. It is my belief that there is no aspect of being Inwardly Sound and Others Focused where the BTA Effect lives more profoundly and detrimentally than in our self-perceptions of how principled we are.

POSSIBILITIES FOR GROWTH

When we combine the BTA Effect with the ability for adults to grow morally and the reality that moral challenges are often not black and white, we recognize the potential to become more principled even within already-principled leaders. Such efforts lead to an even more Inwardly Sound and trustworthy leader.

When leaders are willing to drop the assumption that they are already perfectly principled, they create pregnant opportunities for their own leadership development. But this is far from easy. Admitting that one may not be fully principled is difficult for most leaders (and people!). After spending three months of self-evaluation and growth on being and becoming more principled, a leader whom I respect said,

> *"The hardest lifelong learning for me continues to be the notion that relying on your principles under all circumstances is a true test of character at which I have failed at certain times and in certain situations. Consistent application of principled behavior and action is the difficult part."*

Another outstanding leader who did the same three-month exercise noted,

> *"As leaders we are challenged to be principled every day and every week. Everyday experiences seem to test my commitment to being principled rather than reinforce it. Being principled is hard work!"*

If leaders are able to make those challenges more conscious to themselves, they can be leveraged for exceptional leadership development. But before that can happen, leaders must first be open to the possibility that they have room to improve, even in being principled.

In a few strategic places in this book, I've reserved space for some thoughts that are important but slightly off the beaten path. They are things I often share when I'm speaking in public or coaching leaders in private. To set them apart, I will share them from this, my "soapbox."

Being Inwardly Sound involves more than just being principled. I pause to reiterate this point because too many people want to define great leadership based purely on moral character. Morality plays a role in exceptional leadership, but it's not all that goes into being an Inwardly Sound leader. Becoming a sound vessel—a secure, grounded, trustworthy person both emotionally and relationally—is more complex than simply being principled.

Look again at the five aspects of what makes a leader Inwardly Sound. I put the list in order of importance based on the leadership successes and failures I've observed over the course of my career. Being a principled leader is number three on the list because I've seen many more leadership disasters as a result of the absence of what lives in slots one and two— being secure and settled and being self-aware.

Don't do a disservice to yourself, your organization, your family, your friends, or those who follow you by substituting the fullness of what it means to be Inwardly Sound with the single category of being principled. To do so is to assume you're as well off with one finger on your hand as you are with five.

*3/4 OF YOUR EFFECTIVENESS AS A LEADER COMES FROM WHO YOU ARE, NOT WHAT YOU DO

HOLISTICALLY HEALTHY

RESILIENCE AND CAPACITY IN EACH AREA OF LIFE: PHYSICAL, FINANCIAL, INTELLECTUAL, VOCATIONAL, MENTAL, EMOTIONAL, RELATIONAL, AND SPIRITUAL

Years ago I was leading the development and execution of a multi-day leadership development event. This particular event had been in the works for about nine months. When I arrived on site, my physical energy tank was empty. I'd been neglecting my workouts and eating poorly. In the week leading up to the event, I added a healthy dose of sleep deprivation to the equation.

Not long after arriving at the event, I discovered a small hiccup in the presentations I was to deliver—the visual monitoring system for onstage notes operated differently than I expected. That meant that even as I led the event, I would have to find the time and capacity to re-edit my notes to account for the technology change. In truth, this was a minor inconvenience. But I had little reserve energy, physically or mentally, to deal with it.

As I edited my notes, I repeatedly confused myself. My normal creativity and positive energy were absent. My frustration steadily increased. Then a nudge of panic started growing in me. *Will I be able to pull this off?* became a tangible thought.

Worse yet, when it came to my other leadership responsibilities for the event, I wasn't being what the team needed. As I spiraled into my own little crisis, everything felt like an emergency. For about 48 hours, I operated like a panicked executive, using my authority to influence others to panic as well. The team who needed and expected me to be a rock in the midst of chaos—chaos that is inevitably a part of most large events like this one—now experienced me as a bucket of gasoline to the fires we were managing.

My effectiveness as a leader was deeply compromised. Had I started the event more rested and with months of healthy physical disciplines fueling me, the team I led would have been following a very different leader than the one they got. I would have been the calm voice of reason in the middle of stress and unexpected challenges. Having to edit a few presentations would not have pushed me into self-doubt that spilled out onto our team. (And I would've enjoyed the event far more than I did.)

MULTIPLE BENEFITS

That experience illustrates how holistic health and effective leadership interact. Examples of physical and emotional health are simple enough to understand. But leaders need health and margin in all areas of life—physical, financial, intellectual, vocational, mental, emotional, relational, and spiritual—to be their very best for those they lead.

Fortunately, healthy disciplines often positively affect more than one area of life at a time. For example, Harvard University researcher John Ratey shares that exercise helps more than just your body: "Even if you're in middle age, and you begin to exercise three to four times a week, at fairly moderate rates . . . adding some weights in there . . . you're going to push back cognitive decline by anywhere from 10 to 15 years."[10] That's a physical discipline positively impacting both physical and intellectual health.

Meditation is another example of multiple benefits coming from a single discipline. Studies have shown that meditation can improve high blood pressure (physical health), memory (intellectual and mental health), and attention span (intellectual health).[11] All of these are in addition to the emotional health benefits that initially draw people to the practice.

Healthy relational disciplines such as addressing conflict quickly so as to not let anger and frustration fester can help us mentally by reducing anxiety. And living by healthy financial practices can

DISCIPLINES PRODUCE MARGIN AND MARGIN PRODUCES RESILIENCE AND CAPACITY.

contribute to our emotional and relational health through increased personal security and reduced marital conflict.[12, 13]

Many of us are prone to make excuses for our lack of healthy habits—not having enough time is the most common. But the multifaceted positive affects created by many disciplines invites us to drop the excuses. Holistic health can be pursued efficiently.

WHAT HEALTHY DISCIPLINE PRODUCES

But all that doesn't explain how being holistically healthy makes us more effective leaders. For that, we must look into the dynamics between disciplines, health, margin, resilience, and capacity. As leaders practice disciplines in each area of life, they methodically build up margin. That margin eventually creates two invaluable resources for leaders: resilience and capacity (Figure 8).

Resilience determines how quickly leaders bounce back from problems and overcome obstacles. Capacity enables leaders to take advantage of opportunities that present themselves—even those that don't give a heads-up that they are approaching. Over time, the steady development of resilience and capacity enables consistent engagement and performance by leaders. Personal disciplines fuel long-term, sustainable, high-level performance.

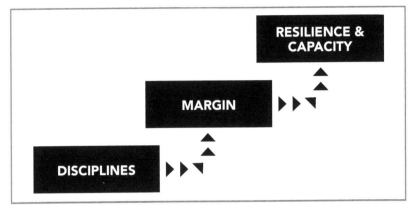

Figure 8: From Disciplines to Resilience & Capacity

For example, when you live by the healthy personal financial disciplines of spending less than you earn and saving money for the future, you build up margin in your bank account. With that margin comes an ability to more easily absorb unexpected expenses (such as a car breaking down). *This* is resilience. That same financial discipline might also allow you to take advantage of an unexpected investment opportunity. *This* is capacity. The presence of personal financial resilience and capacity reduces stress which, in turn, reserves energy for any number of leadership challenges and opportunities that might pop up.

Where leaders choose to institute them, healthy disciplines create resilience and capacity in each area of life—physical, financial, intellectual, vocational, mental, emotional, relational, and spiritual. Even though these disciplines are personal in nature, their positive impact on overall physical, mental, and emotional states gives leaders more resilience and capacity at work as well as at home.

Leaders will always face challenges and opportunities, both expected and unexpected. To deal with them all in a sustainable fashion, leaders must be holistically healthy. Having margin-producing personal disciplines is the pathway to get there.

PURPOSEFUL

BEING INTENTIONAL ABOUT HOW I AM INVESTING MY LIFE AND LIVING IN ALIGNMENT WITH WHAT IS MOST IMPORTANT TO ME

Twenty years ago, developing a personal mission statement was all the rage. It's not so trendy these days, but the idea behind it—the value of clearly defining the purpose of your life—is especially valuable for leaders.

Keep in mind that we're talking about something *personal*—not corporate or organizational goals, mission, or purpose. I'm not talking about hitting quarterly profits or becoming the preferred provider of this, that, or the other thing. Being purposeful is about what you are trying to achieve with your life. It is your personal "Why?"

Maybe it isn't obvious why having a clear purpose and living in alignment with that purpose is beneficial to your followers. After all, isn't your purpose a personal matter—something that doesn't concern or affect those you lead at work or your organization?

Leaders who know why they get out of bed in the morning are stable and focused when it comes to thinking and decision-making. They aren't easily knocked off course. They don't change priorities on a whim. In a world full of ambiguity and uncertainty, this kind of stability is highly valued by followers. It rightly produces trust in the leader. Additionally, when leaders do the hard work of determining what they most want to accomplish and achieve, they often conclude there's more to their work than a bigger paycheck or the next promotion. As they discover and tap into their deeper motives, they become nobler. This attracts and endears followers and fuels respect in the follower-leader relationship.

You would normally find books about your personal purpose in the self-help section of the bookstore. Such texts could easily be placed in the leadership development section as well. Being clear about, taking action toward, and living aligned with your life's purpose provides a steadiness that is both attractive and useful in leadership.

I've had the satisfaction of walking alongside leaders and leadership teams as they work individually to clarify their personal purposes. We do this by not only defining and clarifying what one's purpose is, but even more importantly, creating space for each leader to apply that purpose to real life over the course of a number of months. That means making adjustments to both their schedule and priorities in order to match their stated purpose. The goal in this is to test the purpose in real-life circumstances to determine if it truly aligns with who each individual leader is.

This work, as you might imagine, is often quite personal and sometimes even confronting. What pops out the other side, however, is beneficial not only to the leaders, but also to those they lead. Upon completing the process, one well-developed leader summed it up by saying,

"As a leader, to clarify why I do what I do, what drives me and what my real purpose is, helps provide clarity in direction and decisions. It's motivating to understand this and have this perspective. As a leader, when I understand my purpose, it helps see me through the noise of day-to-day business. People want a leader who is clear, solid, and consistent, and I think being purposeful helps this journey."

EXAMINED VS. UNEXAMINED

Each of the components of being Inwardly Sound can be (and often is) the focus of an entire book, so a detailed investigation of these is beyond the scope of this book. But as you read the descriptions, I suspect you sensed the challenges within each. They have deep connections to the human condition that leaders must be willing to explore within themselves if they are to become healthy, whole, and worth following.

Unfortunately, many leaders can't or won't take on the hard work of their own inner development. The cost of following these leaders is high. After being hit by the shrapnel of leaders who didn't do the work of becoming Inwardly Sound, I no longer naïvely follow them. I avoid following them whenever I can, and when I can't,

AN UNEXAMINED LIFE IS NOT WORTH FOLLOWING.

I brace myself for the confusing priorities and relational gymnastics that are to come. Socrates said, "An unexamined life is not worth living." Perhaps we can add a corollary: "An unexamined life is not worth following."

With that, we've completed our tour of Inwardly Sound. But we're not done digging yet. Now it's time to do the same with being Others Focused.

"Good leaders must first become good servants."
ROBERT GREENLEAF

CHAPTER SIX

Defining What It Means To Be Others Focused

THE WELL-DEVELOPED *WHO*: PART TWO

What is on the mind of a leader each day? Is it the leader's own success, or do the concerns of followers dominate the mind—and perhaps more importantly the heart—of the leader? Is the leader focused on how to get the next promotion or on how to support the current activities and future advancement of those being led? Leaders who are truly Others Focused dedicate themselves to others as a way of life. In many ways, being Others Focused runs counter to our natural self-interest and self-preservation, which is likely why we so rarely see it.

The six components of being Others Focused intertwine with one another and build off of each other. They are less distinct from one another than the components of being Inwardly Sound. That said, none of them are sufficient by themselves; they all need the others in order to complete the picture of being Others Focused.

Just as we did with Inwardly Sound, we will save one of the components of being Others Focused to be addressed in

Chapter 7. The other five we will address here in Chapter 6:

Attentive
Curious
Empathic
Humble
Agapone (ἀγαπῶν)

ATTENTIVE

**BEING FULLY PRESENT TO AND
FULLY ENGAGED WITH OTHERS
IN EVERY INTERACTION**

It's easy—as in massively easy—for leaders to lack attentiveness toward others. Their positions of power invite them and those they lead to live as though the leader is the proverbial center of the universe. It is no wonder that leaders who are consistently attentive to others are the exception rather than the rule.

Leaders who are attentive to others communicate how much they value others. To see this in action, think back to the last time you were telling someone a story and realized midway through that he or she wasn't paying attention. You didn't exactly feel valued in that moment, did you? And that likely didn't endear that person to you either, did it? The relationship between leaders and followers is no different.

Author Parker Palmer says this: "The human soul doesn't want to be advised or fixed or saved. It simply wants to be witnessed—to be seen, heard and companioned exactly as it is."[1] When leaders communicate through actions and words that they are paying attention to more than just themselves or organizational goals, they communicate three simple yet powerful thoughts to those they lead:

You are seen.
You are heard.
You matter.

These ideals satisfy profound human needs. As such, they are deeply motivational. There is great power, therefore, in being a leader who is attentive.

Bob Chapman took over as CEO of US-based Barry-Wehmiller at the age of 30 and subsequently oversaw a 40-year (40 year!) compound annual increase in revenue of 12.8%. That growth moved the company from $20 million (USD) to $2.5 billion (USD) in annual revenue.[2] This was accomplished in part because of Bob's simple yet consequential perspective that "everybody matters." Said Bob, "We've found that a handful of passionate, experienced people can easily outperform any group of so-called stars. All you have to do to unlock their potential is to share a vision of a better future while letting them know they matter, that you value them as full human beings."[3] Giving sincere and focused attention to others is a cornerstone activity of valuing others.

A CAUTION AND THE PAYOFF

Beware of the temptation to try to game the system (i.e., trying to appear attentive when you aren't). Remembering the names and birthdays of the significant others and children of those we lead may seem like a great way to be attentive, but such niceties

*3/4 OF YOUR EFFECTIVENESS AS A LEADER COMES FROM WHO YOU ARE, NOT WHAT YOU DO

will display that leaders are disingenuous if those they lead don't experience genuine attentiveness from them during normal, day-to-day work. Acknowledging, listening to, and prioritizing others in the midst of daily activities is the true test and most valuable aspect of being an attentive leader.

Many of the leaders I consult with know they have work to do when it comes to being attentive. When we begin to dig in on the actual work of becoming more attentive, it feels like they are going for a walk on a cold, rainy day while wearing a coat that is neither waterproof nor warm. They metaphorically drop their heads and put one foot in front of the other with the goal of surviving until we turn our efforts toward a different aspect of leadership three months later.

Because of this, it is especially encouraging to encounter positive stories and examples of being attentive. An executive I worked with for a number of years shared just such a story about a board member for whom she worked.

> *"In an interaction with [the board member], you must be attentive because she is. It is contagious. Maybe this is the biggest takeaway: being truly attentive breeds attentiveness. I'm sure that's true, and it must be good for the workplace in every aspect. More respect, more enjoyment, fewer mistakes, less re-work."*

Those are some awfully valuable outcomes from simply giving others our full attention.

THIEVES OF ATTENTIVENESS

There are two major culprits that can attack and destroy

attentiveness on a minute-by-minute basis. It is the duo of distractions and preoccupations. Many leaders who walk the path of becoming more attentive note that managing distractions is easier than managing preoccupations. So taking a cue from them, let's address distractions first.

There are many forms of distractions that leaders must intentionally manage if they are to value others well. Some are visual. ("Look, there's a squirrel!") Others are auditory. And others are less easily defined. Regardless of their sources, the point is for leaders to notice how, where, and when they get distracted and proactively manage themselves and their environments against those disturbances.

Some leaders with whom I work find their offices to be places of heavy distraction. They discover that having meetings away from their offices—in conference rooms or even off-site—allows them to be far more present with those they lead than they would be if meeting in their offices.

Of course, we can't talk about managing distractions without addressing the issue of the electronics in our lives. Desktop computers, laptop computers, and smartphones all promised to help us be more connected to one another. While that may have happened in a global sense, our electronics have, in many ways, had the opposite effect with the people standing literally right in front of us. Across the world, leaders are missing out on connection with the individuals around them in favor of a relationship with a screen. Little communicates more to followers that they are unimportant, unseen, and unheard than leaders who do not manage their electronics well.

Electronics have become so ubiquitous in our lives that it is now noteworthy when they are absent. The leader who puts away devices and turns off computer screens when followers ask, "Do you have a minute?" is now unique. In this way, it has never been easier for a leader to stand out from the crowd when it comes to being attentive.

From time to time I encounter leaders who insist that they are too busy to give others their full attention. They argue that they have to multi-task—most often using their electronics to do so—in order to merely survive. These leaders often believe that their workload is uniquely challenging. Let me assure you that their circumstances are not unique. (And frankly, even if they were, it doesn't change what it feels like to be on the receiving end of their inattentiveness.) When I encounter these leaders, I tell them the truth that most of them do not want to hear: If you don't have time to give the people you lead your full attention, you don't have time to lead well.

As for preoccupations, the challenge is a bit more complicated. Preoccupations are the ideas, thoughts, and concerns that get ahold of us that we can't seem to shake. Much of our inability to manage them comes from our lack of conscious awareness about them. So simply naming them as a detriment can meaningfully assist your efforts to manage them more intentionally.

Two methods I've seen leaders employ in the management of preoccupations are paper and schedules. Some leaders find success in reducing the noise in their heads created by preoccupations by reserving a spot in their notebooks that is easy to access. When a thought or concern that is off-topic from the current discussion jumps to mind, they simply jot it down in the designated area and come back to it later. Having captured it to be addressed at another time frees them up to stay attentive.

Scheduling is another area where leaders can find success

in being and becoming more attentive. While on the *Who* Not What* journey, some have shared with me that they periodically evaluate their schedules to determine if they are capable of being fully attentive in particular meetings or discussions. If they have a pressing deadline or matter that they know will create a significant preoccupation for them, they schedule meetings and discussions at times in the future, after the pressing issue has been resolved, when they know they can be more fully attentive.

ATTENTIVE VS. AVAILABLE

Managing schedules in order to be more attentive brings up an important point regarding attentiveness. Being 100% attentive does not mean being 100% available. In fact, I would argue that if you are a leader who makes yourself available at all times to those you lead, it will be impossible for you to be 100% attentive. There are simply too many demands on your time and talent for you to completely operate according to everyone else's schedules and priorities. If you do, you will become grossly inefficient in your ability to satisfy the obligations that are uniquely yours. And, on top of that, you will struggle to give people your full attention as you carry

BEING 100% ATTENTIVE DOES NOT MEAN BEING 100% AVAILABLE.

the knowledge, moment by moment, that there are important responsibilities you are not getting to.

There is a balance to be struck here. No one likes to follow a leader that is never available. Never being available communicates the dead opposite of what attentiveness is intended to say to those being led. So it is important that leaders not make their schedules and priorities the only schedules and priorities

*3/4 OF YOUR EFFECTIVENESS AS A LEADER COMES FROM WHO YOU ARE, NOT WHAT YOU DO

that matter. But being 100% available also doesn't work because leaders have their own obligations and priorities to consider. An effective response to a spontaneous request for time that takes everyone into account and supports the leader being fully attentive could be: "I want to be fully attentive to you and the issue you'd like to discuss. But I have some things I'm currently engaged in. Could we meet up later this afternoon [or tomorrow or next week] when I can be fully present?" If followers then get a fully attentive leader when they do meet up, everyone wins.

THE FUNDAMENTAL QUESTION

The details of how to be more attentive, though, can blind us from a critically important question: If you are a leader, do you believe in your heart of hearts that your followers are worthy of your full attention? When investigating being attentive, one executive with whom I work simply said about attentiveness,

> *"It's fundamentally about respecting the other person and treating them with importance."*

Notice that he didn't say that being attentive was fundamentally about making the other person *feel* respected or *feel* important. By focusing on what's happening within the leader, this leader's comment goes to the core of being attentive. The biggest issue is not whether or not followers *feel* important; it is whether or not they *are* important to the leader. If they are, then helping them feel so will not be a difficult task. But if they are not, trying to make them feel as though they are will be a shallow and deceptive act.

Being attentive to others in an impersonal and busy world

is a precious gift leaders have to give. Whether or not they give it is one of the factors that determines if they are leaders worth following.

CURIOUS

(A) PROACTIVELY SEEKING GREATER UNDERSTANDING OF PEOPLE AND SITUATIONS

("Understanding" is not merely intellectual curiosity limited to facts—it includes the perspectives and emotions of others.)

— OR —

(B) LIVING LIFE WITH A PROACTIVE BIAS AGAINST THE ACT OF ASSUMING

Being curious is fundamentally Others Focused. It requires us to take interest in others and their ideas, perspectives, and beliefs. It causes us to proactively ask questions. It demands that we get to know others more deeply than we otherwise would. In its best form, it momentarily puts others at the center of our universe; that produces both good will and new knowledge.

Being curious is fueled by questions, thoughts, and statements such as:

- What else don't I know about him, her, or the situation?
- Tell me more about that.[4]
- What did you mean when you said . . . ?
- Would you mind taking me a little deeper into your thinking on this?

Being curious requires leaders to assume less, judge less, and ask more. Curiosity begins with the unspoken confession that we don't know everything we need to know about people or situations. And, perhaps most difficult, being curious requires us to rid ourselves of judgment. It is impossible to be sincerely curious when we are judging those who see life differently than we do.

RELATIONSHIP + TASK

Both the relational and functional implications of curiosity are valuable. Leaders who consistently dig deeper with their followers build relational capital with them. There's no mystery here: We are all drawn to people who take an interest in who we are and the ideas we have. Functionally, curiosity makes leaders better decision makers because it brings them a fuller and more accurate picture of the choices in front of them.

Most executives and executive teams I work with have to work very hard to discipline themselves against assumption and making snap judgments. Their positional power doesn't require that they ask more questions of those around them. Yet when they do, they are rewarded with better knowledge, better relationships, and better decisions.

Curiosity may have killed the cat, as the saying goes, but it does something much different for leaders who choose it as a lifestyle. Being curious shows others that they are valuable and that we, as leaders, don't already know it all. Both are helpful resources on the path to becoming a well-developed leader.

SURPRISED BY RULO

I had a massive failure in this arena a number of years ago. I was leading a leadership development event for a food distributor in the Southeastern US. I was working side by side with a number of trusted colleagues. Chief among those colleagues was Rulo. If there's ever been a person I could count on, it was Rulo. Willing to stay late? Certainly. Admits mistakes? Yes. Cares about doing a great job? Deeply. Easy to get along with? Definitely. Rulo was a joy to work with.

Near the end of this multi-day event, I asked Rulo about a detail—adding personalized labels to each attendee's thank-you-for-attending gift—that had not yet been executed. Placing these labels would fall to one of our key subcontractors that Rulo was responsible for managing. To be clear, these labels were the very definition of "a detail." They were a nice-to-have element that no one would miss if it weren't completed. In the midst of pulling off something

BEING CURIOUS SHOWS OTHERS THAT THEY ARE VALUABLE AND THAT WE, AS LEADERS, DON'T ALREADY KNOW IT ALL.

as massive as this event, this opportunity would rightly be at the bottom of the list of priorities.

When I asked Rulo about it, I received a very unexpected response. As opposed to the usual, "Absolutely! Whatever it takes!" attitude I'd grown accustomed to over the years from Rulo, I got hesitancy and a lack of openness. I was perplexed and concerned, so I quickly pulled him to the side and re-established our standards. I told Rulo that we needed a different attitude from him. We needed that can-do attitude he'd so consistently displayed as long as I'd known him. Feeling that I had accurately addressed the heart of the matter—Rulo's attitude—I went back to my other duties.

But all was not well.

SCARY WRONG

A number of days later, I learned that my attitude adjustment session had negatively impacted Rulo. He thought he'd been doing yeoman's work (which he had) and that his attitude was anything but the problem. I decided to sit down with him to better understand what had happened.

During the first three days of the event, Rulo had been working hard to manage our relationship with the subcontractor who would have applied the personalized labels. The lines for what we could and couldn't ask from the subcontractor weren't clearly defined in our new contract with them. Not wanting to damage our long-term relationship with this very capable subcontractor or the immediate execution of the event, Rulo had spent the entire event determining moment by moment what was and wasn't worth asking the subcontractor to do. Rulo had been walking a difficult tightrope—a tightrope we wanted and needed him to walk. He had been in a delicate and stressful situation and had handled it with tact and wisdom, just as we would have hoped he would.

Rulo's best assessment was that asking the subcontractor to handle the labels wasn't worth what it would cost relationally. Thus the hesitance and lack of openness I observed. In the moment of my corrective conversation with him, there was neither enough time nor an easy way for Rulo to explain all of this to me. It's no wonder that my attitude-resetting discussion wasn't inspiring or helpful in bringing a key player back in line after a momentary lapse of reason. The only person having a momentary lapse of reason was me.

I COULDN'T ESCAPE MYSELF

Somehow, I was able to see a trusted colleague behaving in an unusual and unexpected way without becoming curious. Instead of leaning into my historical knowledge of Rulo, I decided it was time to re-establish the attitude we needed to succeed. What should have birthed curiosity instead birthed judgment that led to a fracture in our relationship and discouragement for a key player in the midst of a stressful and important moment.

Instead of re-establishing standards, I should have told Rulo what a great colleague he was, shared that his response to the situation was unusual, and asked him if there was anything going on that I should know about. Had I done that, I would have been able to affirm him while learning that he was handling a delicate relational dynamic just as we hoped he would.

As Rulo and I discussed the situation the following week, we came to a simple and embarrassingly obvious conclusion that I needed to learn:

> When something doesn't make sense,
> there's something I don't know.

These are words that I now try to live and lead by. If I want to understand what is really going on when someone's behavior is odd or confusing, I need to get genuinely curious and do so without judgment or assumption.

THE ACTUAL PROBLEM

The biggest problem wasn't that I didn't understand all that was going on; it was that I didn't give Rulo the benefit of the doubt and lean into being curious. In a moment, I magically disregarded years—literally years—of wonderful attitude and behavior from a trusted follower. I ignored mountains of goodwill that Rulo had established.

This problem points to meaningful character flaws in me, the leader: the flaws of judgment, a bent toward believing the worst about someone, and the arrogance of assuming I understood all that was going on.

Who we are as a people always impacts our effectiveness as leaders. In my interaction with Rulo during the event, my underdevelopment as a person kept me from leading well. Those flaws in me had a tangible, significant, immediate, and negative affect on both an important project and an important person.

To be a leader who operates in life with great curiosity is to guard against meaningful negative consequences. But it does much more than that. It also enables us to be more relationally connected to those we lead and to be well informed about the decisions we make.

I have personally mastered few, if any, of the aspects of leadership about which I write. That said, I confess to being exceptionally bad regarding the issue described below. Though not always obvious to others, it is almost always present within me. I was inspired to write this particular soapbox in order to help others avoid the negative leadership repercussions I've seen in my own life due to this shortcoming.

A book that contains the words "Inwardly Sound" and "Humble" wouldn't be complete without addressing one of our most natural and detrimental reactions as humans: defensiveness.

Defensiveness as a reaction to criticism, negative outcomes, and difficult developmental conversations is completely understandable. No one gets excited about hearing how they've fallen short. But just because defensiveness is understandable, that doesn't negate its impact on our leadership. When we're defensive leaders, as many of us naturally are, we severely limit both our opportunities for growth and our emotional connections with those who share feedback with us.

When our first reaction is to explain our choices—that's what we normally call defensiveness—it stymies our ability to hear. Our minds get trapped in mental litigation just as the valuable information flowing out of the mouths of our critics is heading downstream, never to be used for the good it could have produced in us. Even if the other party's assessment of the situation truly is off-base, we still miss valuable information by being defensive. We miss the opportunity to genuinely— and without judgment—understand their perspectives, which would give us a better chance of bringing them over to the reality we see. But those are the rare moments. The far more commonly missed gem is the developmental dialogue that defensiveness eliminates.

On top of that, when our first reaction is to defend the choices we've made, we deny ourselves the blessing of listening without an agenda. When we rid ourselves of the need to be right or understood, we create an openness those critiquing us from the other side of the table feel tangibly. This not only makes way for the feedback we need to hear in order to grow, it also creates a positive emotional connection between us and those sharing the information.

Think about a time when someone fully received your tough feedback by listening intently without being defensive and then asked follow-up questions to completely understand your perspective. How did it make you feel? Hopeful. Connected. Valued. (Unfortunately, you may never have had such a positive experience in sharing difficult feedback.) Those who operate without defensiveness easily separate themselves from the norm in life and leadership by fostering sincere connection between themselves and their critics.

So what is the naturally defensive person to do? Lean in to curiosity. When we become curious, our transformation is no less dramatic than that of a caterpillar to a butterfly. We go from the worst to the best of what we can be. The quality of our relationships follows suit. When we trade defensiveness for curiosity, everyone gets a better deal. We end up with interesting information and healthy relationships rather than an absence of both. When we dedicate ourselves as leaders to being curious, no matter how strong the pull toward defensiveness, we choose the infinitely more valuable path.

Defensiveness is a killer of both personal growth and relationships. To become well-developed people and leaders, we must intentionally watch out for it, and, when it tempts us, choose curiosity instead.

EMPATHIC

STANDING IN OTHERS' SHOES LONG ENOUGH TO
STEP 1   UNDERSTAND THEIR PERSPECTIVES,
STEP 2   FEEL WHAT THEY FEEL, AND
STEP 3   EXPRESS THOSE FEELINGS BACK TO THEM

To best illustrate the value of being an empathic leader, I'd like to introduce you to a young, high-potential leader I know named Jamaal.

Jamaal was working in the manufacturing division of an international beverage conglomerate when he called me with a dilemma. He needed to fire someone . . . who was 40 years older than him . . . over the phone . . . on a different continent. Not an enviable position to be in.

To make matters even more challenging, this was not a circumstance where someone could simply be escorted to the door and have their personal effects mailed to them. The transition needed to go smoothly to protect the company's interests and relationships. This meant that the company needed the person being fired, Lowry, to assist with transitions between himself, his replacement, and the company's clients.

I asked Jamaal to do an exercise to feed his empathy before calling Lowry. I asked him to take a full five minutes—as in actually do it for 300 seconds—to put himself in Lowry's shoes by vividly imagining what it would be like to be Lowry on the other end of the phone. If you were Lowry:

- What would it feel like to receive this call?
- What might race through your mind and heart when you [Lowry] realized the purpose of the call?
- What could this mean for you [Lowry] and your family?
- How would it feel to be fired from across the ocean by someone so much younger than you [Lowry]?
- How might all of this impact your [Lowry's] ego and identity?

Jamaal followed my request and did the exercise before he called Lowry.

ANCHORS AWEIGH

A few days later, I got an update. Jamaal told me that the call with Lowry had gone very well—much better than he had expected it would. Not only had they ended the discussion positively, but it also looked like a healthy transition process would take place.

Weeks later, Jamaal found himself across the ocean and physically in Lowry's presence. They were working together on final transition details. And then Lowry did something unexpected. He invited Jamaal to hang out with him and his wife on their boat.

Wait . . . what?!

That's right. The guy being fired invited the guy firing him to hang out on the guy-being-fired's boat.

Jamaal explained what happened in this way:

> *"When I went through the empathy exercise, the question I tried to answer was, 'How would I want to make my exit?' I tried to feel my way through the various paths I could take and the best way to make him feel good throughout the process. I landed on making it a retirement/goodbye tour. I put myself in his shoes. It was a way for him to save face and go out on a high note with everyone involved, including me. He truly had fun with me the week I was there. This also put us in the best position with the customers as there now wouldn't be any awkward 'What happened with Lowry?' questions."*

Don't mistake this as a story about a smart strategy. That's not where the magic lives. The magic lives in the power of empathy and Jamaal's willingness to be empathic. Lowry was being let go because he needed to be let go. This was termination due to a lack of performance. Despite the pain Lowry had caused with his underperformance, Jamaal was willing to pause to personally feel Lowry's pain. The net result was not merely the strategy Jamaal executed, but the tone and manner in which he handled the entire situation. Everyone involved, including Jamaal himself, felt the positive impact of Jamaal's willingness to empathize with Lowry.

A few months later, I asked Jamaal about the financial impact of his empathy. Jamaal shared that Lowry's smooth exit from the business had protected $3 million (USD) in annual revenue for the company. The power of empathy had extended tangibly from Jamaal's heart to his bottom line.

It is difficult to overestimate the value of empathy in leadership. Few leaders exercise it well because their positional power rarely requires them to do so. They can declare edicts and make demands without having to feel what others are experiencing. Their power invites them to ignore empathy—one of the greatest leadership weapons at their disposal.

Leaders who make genuine empathy a regular part of their emotional lives win. Their sincere interest in others sets them apart from less-developed leaders. The connection forged with others through empathy builds healthy relationships even in—maybe especially in—the toughest of circumstances. (And sometimes it even gets you invited on a boat trip.)

LEADING (AND FOLLOWING) HUMANS

In addition to anecdotal stories and relationship logic that make the case for being an empathic leader, there is research that lauds it as well. A study from one of world's most renowned providers of leadership development, the Center for Creative Leadership, found that empathic leaders earn higher performance evaluations

*3/4 OF YOUR EFFECTIVENESS AS A LEADER COMES FROM WHO YOU ARE, NOT WHAT YOU DO

than those who aren't empathic. This was true in all 38 countries in which their research was conducted.[5]

One of my favorite quotes ever regarding being an empathic leader came from a client (and PhD) who has been in meaningful corporate leadership positions for over a decade. He started out as many do—suspicious of *Who* Not What*. But to his credit, he investigated its data and ideas with genuine openness.

He came to believe in the reality of what the data showed. Today he has personally participated in more *Who* Not What* developmental journeys than any leader I know and has brought *Who* Not What* to many leaders in his organization, including to a number of his frontline leaders.

Given that, his take on being an empathic leader is worth listening to. He simply says,

"Empathy humanizes leadership."

Indeed it does, both for how leaders experience their followers and how followers experience their leaders. Therein lies its powerful role in making leaders effective.

HUMBLE

HAVING A MINDSET OF SELF-FORGETFULNESS, A WILLINGNESS TO SEE AND ADMIT FAULT, AND AN EAGERNESS TO ACKNOWLEDGE OTHERS

Being humble is a keystone quality of exceptional leaders. Next to being secure and settled and self-aware (both from Inwardly

Sound), little else rivals its value within the leader. There is great confusion in the world today about what humility is. Let's start by covering a couple things it isn't.

Humility is not weakness. As humans, we have a natural tendency to make ourselves the central story in our own lives. When unchecked, our minds and hearts fill themselves to the brim with self-interest. Therefore, it takes strength to be humble enough to pull the focus of our lives off of ourselves.

The temptation to be self-consumed applies equally to those who overtly articulate their desires to be catered to—the deep minority of people, in my observation—and to the rest of us who simply allow our minds to quietly focus on our own thoughts and preferences moment by moment, day in and day out.

Secondly, humility is not synonymous with a lack of confidence. If you are capable and talented, having an inaccurate picture of yourself as incapable or untalented doesn't make you humble; it makes you misinformed and potentially a liar (albeit to yourself).

So what *is* humility? And what does it look like to *be* humble? Author C. S. Lewis wrote the most helpful perspective on humility I've encountered.[6] Lewis frames humility as "self-forgetfulness."[7] Inspired by Lewis, co-authors Rick Howard and Jamie Lash wrote, "Real humility is not thinking less of ourselves; it is thinking of ourselves less."[8] That simple sentence points to a wonderfully actionable understanding of humility. At its core, humility is a consistent perspective shift away from self and toward others.

CAPTIVATING AND POTENT

Humility is inarguably an attractive human quality, but why is it so profoundly valuable in leaders? As members of the human race, we long to be (1) valued and (2) connected to a purpose bigger than ourselves. Humility in leaders opens the door to both of these things for followers.

Humble leaders regularly acknowledge with thoughts, words, and actions that they are not the center of the universe. This enables them to more fully value those who follow them even though the leaders' position and authority invite them to do otherwise.

Additionally, humility smooths the path for leaders to connect themselves and their followers to meaningful endeavors because it gets self-focused perspectives out of the way. Humility in leaders enables them to steward their control and power for the sake of followers and important ideals, not just their own egos, enrichment, and advancement. The satisfaction of these two human desires—value and purpose—is why we find humble leaders so captivating and potent.

Humility has other noteworthy characteristics. Stated from the perspective of the leader, humility is . . .

- an awareness that, no matter how hard I have worked, there are positives in my life that others have meaningfully contributed to;
- an appreciation for all others, even those with whom I have significant disagreement;
- a keenness to listen to and learn from others, including those with less education and experience than I have;
- an enthusiasm for giving recognition and praise to others.

Each of these flows out of a desire to take that spotlight off of ourselves and genuinely acknowledge others.

HIDDEN SELF-ORIENTATION

As we consider the role of humility in exceptional leadership, it's worth noting that leaders have power. It's theirs to manage every day. Wherever there's power, the ego is tempted to head in the opposite direction of humility—toward arrogance and pride. It's no surprise, then, that truly humble leaders are infrequently found.

This isn't to suggest that most leaders are chest-thumping, self-promoting egomaniacs. Overt and over-the-top pride is rare because it's socially unacceptable. Most leaders understand that obvious displays of self-interest and self-promotion are distasteful. So they hide their self-orientation inside commitments to organizational objectives. These motives are often so effectively hidden that leaders deceive even themselves about their existence. Leaders believe their desires are purely for the organization's good and that justifies their lack of interest in others' opposing perspectives. As they push toward their own ideas and aspirations, they lack the openness to others' ideas that characterizes truly humble leaders.

Leaders who lack humility aren't evil. They're not even rare. They're the norm. They're you and me. When we aren't regularly humble, we lack what frees us up to have greater interest in and care for the people we're entrusted to lead. When we avoid the trap of **HUMILITY MAKES LEADERS BOTH CAPTIVATING AND POTENT.** daily pride that puts our ideas and interests ahead of others' ideas and interests, it endears our followers to us and feeds exceptional relationships and results.

FOUR LEGS OF THE CHAIR

Humility is difficult to pursue directly as it is primarily about motive and mindset. Doing so can easily devolve into a navel-gazing exercise that produces little shift in perspective or behavior. That's why, in my work with leaders, we come at becoming more humble from four indirect paths. Think of it as the four legs that support the chair called "humble."

From our definition of being humble (page 108) and the bulleted list of humility's characteristics (page 110), you can see two strong themes. The first is gratitude. The second is understanding that we are flawed—we call that "awareness of brokenness." Now add being curious and empathic as discussed previously in this chapter, and we have our four supporting legs.

When we combine curiosity, empathy, gratitude, and awareness of brokenness, we get four statements that support the essence of being humble:

Being curious says, "I don't know everything."
Being empathic says, "I am not the only one that matters."
Having an awareness of my brokenness says, "I am flawed."
Having gratitude says, "I am fortunate."

It is virtually impossible for a leader (or anyone else, for that matter) to consistently and genuinely make these four statements in thoughts, words, and actions and not be humble. When combined, these four truths propel leaders toward a mindset of true humility.

BETTER LEARNING

As I support leaders in their efforts toward greater humility, I'm privy to some very practical stories of growth and progress. One such example came from a senior leader who was focusing on developing greater humility by increasing his awareness of his flaws and errors (awareness of brokenness).

His team was involved in an international acquisition. Because his antennas were raised a bit higher than normal for seeing his contributions to problems and taking responsibility for them, when his team ran into a problem, he proactively shared with them where he thought he had dropped the ball.

> *"Once I began talking about my contribution to the issue, the guarded nature of my team dropped. I then 'gut-fully' owned my part, and in response the team surprisingly communicated that I had contributed to the problems differently than I thought I had. My self-reflection was more off the mark than on, and they let me know. Thankfully, I was in a state of grace to discuss it and own my part. In that mental state, when the curveball came my way via different feedback than I was expecting, I was able to receive it without pushback. I actually appreciated it. The state of mental grace I was in allowed me to accept and understand my contribution to the problem more than I would have in a different mental state. This gave me greater learning and growth from the experience."*

What happens to those following this senior leader when they see him owning his errors and even remaining open to hear that it was actually different than he thought? Do they back away in fear or engage more? Engage more, of course, just as they did. And when they did, learning and development increased for the senior leader. Not only that, but anyone involved who might be

*3/4 OF YOUR EFFECTIVENESS AS A LEADER COMES FROM WHO YOU ARE, NOT WHAT YOU DO

wondering, *What's the best way to maximize the value of feedback in my own development?* got their answer by watching his example. It was, *With humility.*

Humility is one of the most attractive and effective qualities a leader can have. Across the gamut of leadership activities, from cultivating talent to crafting strategy, it supports and enables exceptional outcomes.

AGAPONE (ἀγαπῶν)

SERVICE TO AND CARE FOR OTHERS THAT IS SELFLESS, CONSISTENT, AND UNCONDITIONAL

This word in English is pronounced ah-gah-pone. It is derived from "agape," one of the Ancient Greek words that translates into English as "love."[9] The Greeks understood that loving a candy bar, a sibling, and a lover are not the same thing. So they used different words for different types of love. Agapone translates literally as "being unconditionally loving."

Agapone, in its most basic sense, is about the decision to serve others and care for them as a way of being. I use the word "decision" here quite intentionally. Agapone is less about a feeling and more about a commitment to how to think about and treat others. It is about action born from a conviction from within.[10] In this regard, the word "love" in English can be misleading and distracting, as in the English language "love" is almost always tied to emotion rather than action. Sometimes the English language fails us by not having a broader set of words to give nuance where needed. Regardless of the English language's shortcomings, agapone delivers concern for, dignity to, and respect to others no matter the circumstances.

I suppose it can be uncomfortable to talk about "care" or "love" in a corporate setting. But would you rather follow a leader who loves you or one who doesn't? Who will get more out of you as a follower—the leader who cares about you as person or the leader who doesn't? We simply must force ourselves to talk about agapone. To ignore it would be to ignore something that has nearly limitless potential for leaders.

How do you know if you're becoming an agapone leader—a leader who cares and serves? Robert Greenleaf, former AT&T executive and the founder of the modern-day servant leadership movement, said,

> "The servant leader is servant first. . . . That person is sharply different from one who is leader first. . . . The difference manifests itself in the care taken by the servant-first to make sure that other people's highest priority needs are being served. The best test, and difficult to administer, is: Do those served grow as persons? Do they, while being served, become healthier, wiser, freer, more autonomous, more likely themselves to become servants?" [11]

The pointed and challenging question is this: As we look at those we lead over time, are they progressing as Greenleaf articulated?

FROM THOSE ON THE JOURNEY

The insights realized by executives who pursue *Who* Not What* development are a wonderful source of learning regarding agapone. As they intentionally engage with the idea in the midst of the live ammunition of everyday leadership, their observations exceed what can be gleaned from a single conversation or meeting. Here are a few of their thoughts after having worked on being and becoming more agapone over a four month period.

> ". . . thinking about the needs of others around you—how you are accommodating those, or not—and making a deliberate decision about that in order to maximise engagement and satisfaction—and therefore advance the organization—makes excellent sense."

> "It [agapone] gives you connection with your people. It makes you think about how well do you really know and understand the people you work with. . . . You can't fake care and interest; it has to come from the heart."

> ". . . it is important to treat everything around you as a gift that you do not want to squander."

> "While there are many other reasons that garner loyalty, agapone certainly ranks up there to gain followers. At the same time, agapone creates a good bit of loyalty from the leader to the follower so it is circular in a way. Roll this all together and you get a more effective leader."

Another executive I was working with on being more agapone spoke about wanting to avoid a difficult conversation that was essential for the other person's development. In a very simple yet important application point, he said:

"Agapone requires me not to prioritize my own comfort above their needs."

And there you have it: selfless service to others.

It is important to understand that agapone is not about an exchange. It is not *quid pro quo*. It is the opposite of that. It is serving and giving without the requirement of reciprocity. That is the very thing that elevates the leader/follower relationship from an exchange of time, talent, and effort for money to something far more valuable, productive, and fulfilling for all parties involved.

EVERYONE'S WATCHING

One leader with whom I've worked consciously put agapone into action by working on behalf of someone who was leaving her team. An employee chose to move to a different division of the company. Despite the leader's belief that the move was not a good choice for the employee, the leader did everything in her power to ensure that the employee was appropriately taken care of financially in the process of making the move. The leader was expending energy to care for someone who would not be paying her back with effort or loyalty. And yet, she took advantage of the moment to exercise and practice being agapone.

But here's a little secret to know: everyone else was watching. I hesitate to tell you this lest you be tempted to give to others in order to be recognized as a giver. (By the way, a giver who looks for praise for giving is not 100% purely giving.) But the truth is that people are always watching the leader. They want to know if the leader is trustworthy. They want to know if the leader cares about them personally. That leads us to note two types of transitions followers can't help but watch intently: firings and layoffs.

FIRINGS, LAYOFFS, AND AGAPONE

At first glance, firings and layoffs appear to be antithetical to being agapone. After all, how could a leader be serving and caring for people while removing them from their livelihoods? To start, if firings and layoffs are the first levers pulled when financial or performance pressures arise, it is a clear sign that being agapone is lacking. While firings and layoffs can produce significant positive financial effects, they are often personally devastating to those who are let go and have the potential to severely damage trust between leaders and the followers who remain.

So when exactly are firings and layoffs not in opposition to being agapone?

Individually, people need to be held accountable for their performance over time. If they are not, their growth, the credibility of the leader, and the opportunity to maximize the potential of the organization are all at risk. If—and this is a monumentally big "if"—proper training, sufficient time, adequate tools, and constructive feedback have been supplied, it is not serving of leaders to look the other way when poor performance shows up. It is not caring to allow followers to consistently underperform without receiving progressively significant consequences.

If leaders don't set standards and hold followers to them, they enable mediocrity (or worse) and influence everyone around them to be less than they are capable of being. In those situations, the organization needs better performance, and the individual needs to hear a message that isn't getting through via other means. Thus, as a final choice—after myriad options have been exercised—letting someone go can fall under the banner of 'tough love' that is not in opposition to being agapone and supports the long-term interests of both the organization and the person being fired.

Organizationally, there are times when increased competition, new technologies, geopolitical events, or other forces push leaders to reduce the size of their organizations in order to preserve their companies' long-term viability and health. Let me reiterate that if layoffs are one of the first levers pulled, agapone—and strategic creativity as well—are missing. That said, I don't think we could call it agapone if leaders put the entire company at risk because they are unwilling or unable to follow through with needed layoffs.

When circumstances dictate that firings or layoffs occur, we are reminded of a key truth about the *Who* * *Not What Principle*: Much of the time, understanding *Who* * *Not What* does not change what needs to be done but instead determines how it can best be done. Taking into account the existence of *Who* * *Not What* means that leaders need to be agapone in the midst of firings and layoffs. While it is virtually impossible to go through layoffs without damaging at least some trust with followers, the trust that remains within those who are not laid off can vary wildly depending on how the layoffs are handled. Even well-deserved firings hold within them the opportunity for the leader be agapone.

I have witnessed firsthand the phenomenon of an agapone leader gaining trust and respect by how a follower was fired. In this instance, an individual was being fired for an egregious safety decision. Frankly, he deserved to be treated with the bare minimum as he was shown the door. But in the spirit of agapone, the leader in charge insisted on being more respectful and financially considerate of the guilty party than was required. In that, I saw the epitome of the unconditional nature of agapone. And my trust and respect grew for the leader doing the firing.

MUCH OF THE TIME, UNDERSTANDING *WHO* NOT *WHAT* DOES NOT CHANGE WHAT NEEDS TO BE DONE BUT INSTEAD DETERMINES HOW IT CAN BEST BE DONE.

As for layoffs, agapone can reveal itself in a variety of ways. From the methods by which the news is shared to the tone of messages delivered to the follow-on support offered, agapone has the power to communicate service and care for others even as they are being laid off. This isn't to suggest that the people being let go will be happy with the leaders doing it. But the blow can be lessened by how humanely and generously it is delivered. And that can reduce the loss of trust—though certainly not eliminate it—with those who remain in the organization.

Individual firings and organizational layoffs can be implemented by leaders in an agapone manner when they're reluctantly and carefully executed. Are the people leaving the organization treated with the utmost respect and care as they are moved on from the organization? Are they given every reasonable financial consideration as they exit? Does communication with them reflect concern for what is happening to them? Leaders who wish to be agapone in these circumstances must find ways to serve and care even as they move people out of the organization.

To reiterate, everyone is always watching the leader. They are not solely watching the decisions that are made; they are also watching how the leader operates in the midst of those decisions. In all circumstances—most especially those where people are being let go—followers are watching to see whether being agapone is at the core of the leader or not.

CONTROL FREAKS CELEBRATE

For the control freaks reading this, the last word in the definition of agapone should be one you love. That word is "unconditionally." This means that no matter whether our followers deserve dignity, care, and respect, we choose to give it to them. (That doesn't mean we put thieves in charge of the safe. See the next soapbox for more about that.) When agapone is present in us, our followers' actions are not in control of how we as leaders treat them. We are.

In an odd way, despite how difficult it can be to serve and care for others who are, at times, not easy to serve or care for, agapone is freeing. It says, "This is how I'm going to interact with you no matter how you interact with me." It says, "This is who I am going to be no matter who you are going to be." It says, "There is nothing a follower can do to derail how I, the leader, have committed to treat you. I, the leader, am in charge of me, and agapone is how I choose to be." (Control freaks celebrate!)

HEADING SOUTHWEST

Southwest Airlines is known for something every company in the world wants to be known for: creating profits. For 45 years in a row and counting, Southwest Airlines has been profitable. Impressive without any other adornment, the accomplishment

*3/4 OF YOUR EFFECTIVENESS AS A LEADER COMES FROM WHO YOU ARE, NOT WHAT YOU DO

increases in stature when you consider that Southwest resides in the airline industry—an industry known for financial losses and bankruptcy filings.

From its humble beginnings as a regional carrier in Texas, Southwest intentionally fashioned itself as a company dedicated to developing leaders with the heart to serve those they lead. Herb Kelleher, founder of the company said, "Show [people] that you admire, value, and love them as individuals, rather than just as 'producers.' . . . Your people [employees] come first, and if you treat them right, they'll treat the customers right."[12]

Kelleher's servant philosophy of leadership helped grow the business from profits of $34 million (USD) in 1981 to $511 million (USD) 2001.[13] After 21 years at the helm, Kelleher stepped aside for Colleen Barrett to become President.[14] Barrett's appointment was noteworthy for two reasons. First, there were few female executives in the airline industry at the time. Second, Barrett had begun her tenure at Southwest Airlines as a legal secretary.

> "SHOW [PEOPLE] THAT YOU ADMIRE, VALUE, AND LOVE THEM AS INDIVIDUALS, RATHER THAN JUST AS 'PRODUCERS.'" — HERB KELLEHER, FOUNDER OF SOUTHWEST AIRLINES

Just a few months into Barrett's presidency, the 9/11 terror attack struck. What would she do in the face of massive downward financial pressures brought on by an industry-wide tragedy? Rather than laying off employees, Southwest renegotiated its airline contracts. When coupled with its already finely tuned organizational structure that was underwritten by the cultural spirit of the company, renegotiating airline contracts was enough to do the trick. In the 4th quarter of 2001, immediately after 9/11, without laying off one employee or reducing their pay, Southwest turned a profit.[15]

Said Southwest Airlines Senior Vice President Linda Rutherford of Barrett, "Her interest, first and foremost, was serving our employees. The way she navigated that tragic event was a pivotal moment in the airline industry and just one example of her incredible leadership."[16]

In a speech after her retirement, Barrett said, "When employees have a problem, or when we have employees that see a passenger having a problem, we adopt them, and really work hard to make something optimistic come out of whatever the situation is."[17]

Southwest's presidents following Barrett, Gary Kelly and Tom Nealon, have continued with the airline's commitment to leaders who embody being agapone. For its efforts, Southwest has continued its more than 20-year run as one of *Fortune* magazine's "Most Admired Companies"[18] and has eclipsed $1 billion (USD) in profits for each of the last 5 years.[19]

For those who feel squeamish talking about love, care, and a servant's heart in business, it's not just Southwest's leadership philosophy that will challenge you. So will the company's ticker symbol on the New York Stock Exchange. It's LUV.

Agapone within leaders elevates the relationship between leader and follower far beyond a mere transaction. Its presence over time elicits the very best from those we lead and thereby produces exceptional results. Though it may not be comfortable or common to pursue being agapone, we simply must. To avoid it for any reason would be to neglect a crucial quality of *Who* that makes the very best leaders worth following.

Using parent-child examples for leadership education is dangerous because it invites leaders to view the adults they lead as children, which they are not. But I'm going to use one parent-child example now and hope it doesn't get misused.

Some people hear the word "love" and conclude that living out agapone means ignoring missed deadlines, letting sub-standard performance go unchecked, and giving hugs at the company picnic. Nothing could be further from the truth. While agapone does require the leader to consider concepts like grace, compassion, forgiveness, and consideration toward followers, it does not mean doing so with one's head in the sand.

Would you call it "loving" for parents to never correct their children? Would you consider it caring if parents never communicated any standards of conduct to their kids? Our job as leaders is not to be a parent to our adult followers, but it is to develop and grow them, to help them achieve more individually and as a group than they could have without our leadership. Just as the best parents use the long-term development and wellness of their children as the driving force behind their day-to-day parenting decisions, the best leaders think about the long-term best interests of their followers as a guide for how to handle difficult situations and opportunities for development.

You wouldn't hand a bag of cookies for safekeeping to a child who had just been caught with his hand in the cookie jar. Nor should you look the other way at poor performance or behavior from your followers. Doing so isn't unconditionally loving. It's enabling conduct that will hurt your followers in the long run. To allow poor performance and behavior in the name of "love" is anything but loving.

RELISHING OTHERS

As with the components of being Inwardly Sound, each aspect of being Others Focused is worthy of investigation beyond what is offered here. That said, I trust you now have a good feel for how valuable, effective, and challenging it can be to be a leader who is Others Focused.

We've all had moments when we realized we were thinking completely about ourselves, even if we were doing it by accident. This happened to me not all that long ago. I had many people around me asking about how I was holding up as I led the development of a complex learning experience for a large group of leaders. I shared in self-indulgent detail the ups and downs of preparing for the big event.

Then one morning, as I sat at my desk, the light bulb switched on. I thought of my recent conversations and realized just how self-consumed I'd become. As others inquired about my wellness and work, I took almost no interest in theirs. It was particularly embarrassing considering the focus of the big event was—that's right, you guessed it—being Others Focused. If we are to reach our potential as leaders, we must resist temptations to be self-interested and instead become the type of people who relish giving care to, having concern for, and taking interest in our followers.

In the business world, this reality has been measured. A Towers Watson study found that an important driver of employee engagement is whether or not senior leaders are Others Focused. Of employees whose survey answers identified them as "highly engaged," 74% said their senior leaders were "interested in their employees' well-being." That number plummeted to 44%, 28%, and 18% for employees whose survey answers identified them as "unsupported," "detached," and "disengaged," respectively.[20] Such data points directly to the value of being a leader who is Others Focused. For anyone who might be concerned about the causality between engagement and the perception of leadership effectiveness—does effective leadership drive engagement or does engagement drive the perception of leadership effectiveness? Towers Watson clarified that issue with a clear and direct statement: "Leadership has been a primary driver of employee engagement for as long as we have studied it."[21]

When combined with being Inwardly Sound, being Others Focused creates a steadfast trust between followers and leaders. Little else is as valuable to leaders, followers, and the endeavors in which they engage than trust. It's the grease that keeps organizations and teams running smoothly and without friction.

MEET COACH KEADY

Leadership and trust are often cited as keys to success in the world of athletics. During player and coach interviews, as the confetti falls after a championship win, leadership and trust often enter into the discussion.

I've spent a sizable chunk of my life in and around college athletics. I grew up hanging around a college football training room. My father was part of the medical staff for West Virginia University's athletic department and football team for 40 years. My brother is a Division I men's head basketball coach, formerly for the US Military Academy (West Point) and currently at Drexel University. Though not formally employed in college athletics, my mother and sister often have ESPN on in the background of their daily activities—especially on Saturdays in the Fall.

I not only spent my first two years of college as an electrical engineering student at Purdue University, but I also "played" for the school's basketball team. The quotation marks are there because I'm using the broadest possible definition of "played." I was a non-scholarship player (also known as a "walk-on") who, over the span of two seasons, logged a total of 27 minutes of game time . . . if you round up.[22] A college basketball game is 40 minutes long. So, many of my teammates played more in one game than I did during my entire career at Purdue.

That said, being on the team at Purdue helped shape me. It taught me about excellence. It taught me about pushing myself to my physical and mental limits. And it taught me what trust underwritten by a well-developed leader can produce.

Our coach was Gene Keady.

IF WE ARE TO REACH OUR POTENTIAL AS LEADERS, WE MUST RESIST TEMPTATIONS TO BE SELF-INTERESTED AND INSTEAD BECOME THE TYPE OF PEOPLE WHO RELISH GIVING CARE TO, HAVING CONCERN FOR, AND TAKING INTEREST IN OUR FOLLOWERS.

He's a legendary figure in Purdue basketball history. The son of a Kansas florist, Keady is the school's all-time winningest head coach with 512 wins. During his 25 years at Purdue, he tallied 6 National Coach of the Year awards, 6 Big Ten regular season championships, 7 Big Ten Coach of the Year awards, and 17 NCAA Tournament appearances. Keady holds a 40-2 record in a variety of coaching roles representing the United States in international competition including being an assistant coach for the gold-medal-winning US Men's Basketball team at the 2000 Olympic games in Sydney. In 2007 he was given the prestigious Legends of Coaching Award. And in 2013 he was inducted into the National Collegiate Basketball Hall of Fame. [23, 24, 25]

Keady also has an impressive coaching tree. Between assistant coaches, players, and managers, the team I played on at Purdue produced no fewer than five Division I head coaches.[26] That team also included the first pick in the 1995 NBA draft, Glenn Robinson. (Okay, that last point was gratuitous, but when you play as little as I did, you have no choice but to take solace in your teammate's accomplishments.)

Keady was a what-you-see-is-what-you-get leader. I'm not sure I've ever met someone so comfortable with himself.[27] If you needed to hear something, he said it without hesitation. And he didn't dance for the media. He simply told them how things were from his perspective.

He had a public reputation as a fiery competitor, but he was more than that. Behind his scowl was a guy who laughed, loved coaching, and seemed to enjoy teaching us about more than just basketball.

I remember looking in a store window near campus one day. Inside the display was a T-shirt that read, "Keady's Kids." Below those words were 13 tiny basketballs, each displaying the jersey number of one of the players on our team. I bought the shirt because the term "Keady's Kids" struck me as accurate. Decades later, it still strikes me that way.

I learned constantly while playing basketball for Gene Keady. We started each practice with a life lesson that may or may not have had anything to do with basketball. There was discipline—lots and lots of discipline. By that I don't mean discipline problems (though we occasionally had some of that). I mean learning the physical and mental disciplines of playing competitive Big Ten basketball. And there was love. I felt it from Keady. His affection for us as players was obvious. The thought never once crossed my mind that he was coaching us in order to get rich, exercise a need for power, or stroke his ego. He was comfortable with who he was, and he cared about his players.

YOU'RE INCLUDING ME? REALLY?

After my sophomore year, I transferred to complete my engineering studies and basketball career at Division III Washington University in St. Louis. As I left, Purdue began a string of three consecutive outright regular season Big Ten championships, a feat that has been achieved only one other time since the Big Ten began playing basketball in 1906.[28]

In the Spring after Purdue won the last of its three-peat Big Ten championships, I received a package in the mail. Inside the package was a very nice Purdue basketball golf shirt and a letter. The letter explained that Purdue's recent success was, in part, a function of a basketball program built by its former players. So, as part of Gene Keady's latest contract with Nike, he had

I WAS A WALK-ON WHO BARELY PLAYED AND THEN TRANSFERRED TO ANOTHER SCHOOL. AND I WAS BEING INCLUDED IN THIS? REALLY? WOW.

included a clause that required Nike to send a piece of Purdue basketball swag to all of its former players on an annual basis. I read that letter and sat down in my living room amazed. I was a walk-on who barely played and then transferred to another school. And I was being included in this? Really? Wow.

Next, I wondered how many Division I coaches would even think about doing what Gene Keady did in his contract with Nike. It's said you can tell a lot about a person by how they treat those who have nothing to give them in return. Most former athletes have little to offer their collegiate sports programs once they've graduated. Yet Gene Keady included us in his and his team's recent success. Wow, again.[29]

In 1998, I was invited with hundreds of others to attend a roast of Coach Keady. It was an opportunity to celebrate him and see many former teammates, so I made the drive from St. Louis to West Lafayette.

At the end of the evening, I spoke briefly with Coach. He thanked me for coming. I tried to shrug off the thank you, but he stopped me, looked me dead in the eye, and said, "No, Timmy. Seriously. Thank you for coming." It was such a heartfelt thank you that I still remember it today, more than 20 years after it happened. Again, I was a walk-on who played 27 minutes in two seasons before transferring to another school to finish my college career. To say I had nothing to offer Gene Keady is a gross understatement. Yet he made sure I got the message of his gratitude loud and clear.

There is an interesting sub-story to Gene Keady's tenure as head coach at Purdue. Under Keady's leadership, Purdue routinely finished higher in the Big Ten standings than predicted. From firsthand experience, I believe Keady's teams outperformed expectations because of one word: effort. Purdue's teams were known for playing hard. In fact, the words "PLAY HARD" were screen printed on the back of every player's practice shorts. And we did . . . but not solely because Keady expected it from us. He earned our effort. He wasn't there to fill his bank account or feed his ego. He was there for us and we knew it. Keady was Inwardly Sound and Others Focused. He was trustworthy. Because Gene Keady was who he was, he got more out of his players than others thought possible. And that won more games than people expected for 25 years.

We've now looked in detail at being Inwardly Sound and Others Focused. But we're not ready to move on just yet. It's time for us explore one final quality of being a well-developed *Who* that uniquely combines aspects of both Inwardly Sound and Others Focused.

"Our feelings are not there to be cast out or conquered. They're there to be engaged and expressed with imagination and intelligence."

T.K. COLEMAN

CHAPTER SEVEN

One More Thing

THE WELL-DEVELOPED *WHO*: PART THREE

In each of the previous two chapters, I mentioned that there was a component of being a well-developed *Who* that we would wait until Chapter 7 to address. Well, here we are. In both instances, I was referring to the same component of being a well-developed *Who*: emotionally mature.

The concept of being emotionally mature is unique in that it requires leaders to be well-developed in specific aspects of both Inwardly Sound and Others Focused. (Precisely which ones, we'll get to later in this chapter.) Being emotionally mature is, therefore, part of *both* Inwardly Sound *and* Others Focused. It is the only component of being a well-developed *Who* that has this quality. You can see this represented in Figure 9 on page 134.

When I began writing this book, I didn't expect to dedicate an entire chapter to the concept of being an emotionally mature leader. Though I know it is a critical leadership issue, it is not more valuable than what we've already explored in Chapters 5 and 6. But when I actually started writing, there was so much to share that it didn't fit into either of those chapters.

Yes, you'll hear references that draw on ideas from Chapters 5 and 6. But because of the unique concoction that is emotional

THE WHO OF LEADERSHIP

OTHERS FOCUSED

ATTENTIVE

CURIOUS

EMPATHIC

HUMBLE

AGAPONE (ἀγαπῶν)

EMOTIONALLY MATURE

INWARDLY SOUND

SECURE + SETTLED

SELF-AWARE

PRINCIPLED

HOLISTICALLY HEALTHY

PURPOSEFUL

Figure 9: The Who of Leadership

maturity, you need not be concerned that we will repeat what we've already covered. In fact, there's reason to be excited as we look into this topic: Leaders who have gone on *Who* Not What* journeys rate their work on becoming more emotionally mature as the most valuable aspect of their entire *Who* Not What* expedition. So, with that as our backdrop, let's get to the definition of being emotionally mature and begin to explore its realities.

EMOTIONALLY MATURE

RECOGNIZING AND RESPONDING TO MY EMOTIONS AND THE EMOTIONS OF OTHERS IN WAYS THAT INCREASE ENERGY, CONNECTION, INFLUENCE, AND INFORMATION[1]

Much has been written, and rightly so, about the leadership impact of handling emotions well. Emotionally mature leaders are vigilant about the emotional states of themselves, those they lead, and the organization at large. In doing so, they avoid the sideways energy that is fed when leaders ignore or don't see the presence and importance of emotion.

Emotional maturity is the ability to understand our emotions and the emotions of others and use that understanding for the benefit of the people and projects we lead. It's being aware of how our emotions affect others. It's observing others' emotions and understanding what those emotions are communicating. And it's helping others understand and handle their own emotions deftly with consideration for themselves, their fellow laborers, and their organizations.

Like it or not, if you are in a position of leadership in any type of organization from a family at home to an international corporation, you are never merely the leader of strategy and execution. You are always also, and often more importantly, the leader of emotion. To ignore this reality is to miss one of leadership's most critical responsibilities and greatest points of leverage.

YOU ARE NEVER MERELY THE LEADER OF STRATEGY AND EXECUTION. YOU ARE ALWAYS ALSO, AND OFTEN MORE IMPORTANTLY, THE LEADER OF EMOTION.

Emotionally mature leaders understand that it is never enough to ask themselves, "What do I want my people to know and do?" They know they must also ask themselves, "What do I want my people to feel?" and then take action to make it happen.

FROM LEADER TO PERFORMANCE

Much has been made over the last 25 years about the value of being emotionally mature. No one is more responsible for that movement than Daniel Goleman. Goleman is famous for using the terms "emotional quotient" and "emotional intelligence."[2] I purposely use "emotional maturity" here in order to ensure we are talking about more than an intellectual understanding of emotions. In order to be emotionally mature, leaders must strongly value emotions and find concrete actions that support that value.

Goleman, along with co-authors Richard Boyatzis and Annie McKee, wrote *Primal Leadership*. In it, they draw clear connections between emotion and performance.

". . . Consider the results of a study of sixty-two CEOs and their top management teams.[3] The CEOs represented some of the Fortune 500, as well as leading U.S. service companies (such as consulting and accounting firms), not-for-profit organizations, and government agencies. The CEOs and their management team members were assessed on how upbeat—energetic, enthusiastic, determined—they were. They were also asked how much conflict and tumult the top team experienced, that is, personality clashes, anger and friction in meetings, and emotional conflicts (in contrast to disagreement about ideas).

"The study found that the more positive the overall moods of people in the top management team, the more cooperatively they worked together—and the better the company's business results. Put differently, the longer a company was run by a management team that did not get along, the poorer that company's market return."[4]

As leaders influence the emotions of those they lead, whether intentionally or unintentionally, they influence their performance. And who do you imagine commonly has the most emotional influence in the room? Let's hear from Goleman and company again.

"Because the leader's way of seeing things has special weight, leaders "manage meaning" for a group, offering a way to interpret, and so react emotionally to, a given situation.[5]

*3/4 OF YOUR EFFECTIVENESS AS A LEADER COMES FROM WHO YOU ARE, NOT WHAT YOU DO

"But the impact on emotions goes beyond what a leader says. In these studies, even when leaders were not talking, they were watched more carefully than anyone else in the group. When people raised a question for the group as a whole, they would keep their eyes on the leader to see his or her response. Indeed, group members generally see the leader's emotional reaction as the most valid response, and so model their own on it—particularly in an ambiguous situation, where various members react differently. In a sense, the leader sets the emotional standard."[6]

The leader is the most emotionally influential person in the room. We must be conscious of this if we are to be leaders worth following. As a humorous (and somewhat sad) anecdote, I have in my possession a photo taken at a session where a colleague of mine was teaching about the emotional influence of leaders. In the background of the photo is the president of the company standing separated from the group with his eyes glued to his phone. What emotions do you think he inspired in his people in that moment? And if those emotions were sustained over time through similar actions from the president and other executive leaders, is there any chance that organization would reach its full potential? Not likely.

FOUR COMPONENTS AND FOUR STEPS

As we survey the various aspects of being Inwardly Sound and Others Focused, being emotionally mature does not show up by itself. Instead, it is comprised of four components of being a well-developed *Who*, two from Inwardly Sound and two from Others Focused. Broken down precisely, it looks like this:

Being emotionally self-aware
(part of Inwardly Sound: Self-Aware)

+

Being emotionally healthy
(part of Inwardly Sound: Holistically Healthy)

+

Being aware of the emotions
and emotional states of others
(part of Others Focused: Attentive)

+

Being empathic toward others
(part of Others Focused: Empathic)

=

Being Emotionally Mature

As you can see, emotional maturity has equal footing in both being Inwardly Sound and being Others Focused. Thus we've saved it to be addressed here once all other aspects of being Inwardly Sound and Others Focused have been addressed.

Emotional maturity leans heavily on an intellectually simple understanding of life's events (Figure 10 on page 140). Our immediate, internal reactions are the thoughts and feelings that are automatically triggered when something happens to us. They are what we experience upon engaging with stimuli. In the very short term, these are not things we can control. It is what first ran through your mind and heart when you discovered a colleague had taken credit for your idea. It is what you immediately felt when you learned you got the big promotion. It is the gut-level reaction you had when you learned that your high schooler had once again gotten picked up by the police.

What happens after the immediate, internal reaction is what determines whether or not the leader is emotionally mature. Is there recognition of the fact that there is a choice to make after the immediate, internal reaction? If so, you are stepping toward emotional maturity.

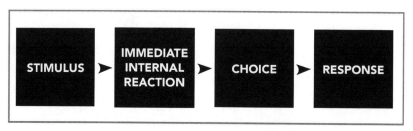

Figure 10: Process of Emotions

Emotional immaturity—and the subsequent relational inefficiency that accompanies it—shows up when leaders lose sight of the fact that they have a choice about what they do with their immediate, internal reactions. When leaders submit themselves to their own emotional reactions rather than choosing to make conscious choices regarding their emotions, they never actually make it to a response. And their organizations become less healthy and ineffective because of it.

GETTING TO RESPONSE

Thankfully, there are ways to become more emotionally mature. Specifically, there are four actions to lean into when it comes to being and becoming more emotionally mature: (1) recognize our own emotions, (2) respond to our own emotions, (3) recognize others' emotions, and (4) respond to others' emotions.

It is my observation and estimation that 2/3 of emotional maturity is about dealing with self. If we can recognize our own emotions and consciously choose how to respond to them, we will have covered a great deal of what emotional maturity is all about. But doing so is not a given. It takes intentionality and energy that is rarely championed in families or organizations.

At times, emotional maturity can feel like a complicated issue. With so many people and so many emotions—most especially emotions that do not overtly present themselves— is it even possible that the emotions of life and work can be consistently dealt with in a constructive, mature, and even productivity-enhancing fashion? Yes. But how?

The first answer lives in a place where one might not expect to find emotion: science. Neuroscience has shown that the rise and fall of the physiological effects of emotion takes six seconds.[7] Therefore, one simple method for becoming more emotionally mature is for us to slow ourselves and others down when we are emotionally triggered. When we do this, we give our physiology an opportunity to run its course, which then allows us to consciously and intentionally respond to stimuli rather than merely react to them.

This slowing down is not only about stopping us from making rash statements or committing career limiting mistakes. It is also about leading effectively in a world full people with legitimate emotional needs—ourselves included. Sometimes, the most emotionally mature action we can take is to let our emotions be seen and felt by others. On the other hand, sometimes we need to reserve our external show of emotion for a later time and place. The best answer can change situation by situation. But what does not change is the importance of getting ourselves and those we lead to cease being ruled by our immediate, internal reactions and instead make conscious choices about how we will respond to emotions. Slowing down—even just for six seconds—helps immensely with this.

The second answer for how to be more emotionally mature in an emotionally complex world resides in the four outcomes listed in our definition of being emotionally mature: connection, energy, influence, and information. Each group of leaders I work with in their *Who* Not What* journeys is asked to, over the course of four months, consciously choose responses to emotion that will increase (1) their connection with their followers, (2) energy in their followers, (3) their influence with their followers, and (4) the flow of information between them and their followers. Even when the why behind emotions is a tangled mess of complexity, focusing on choices that increase these four outcomes simplifies and illuminates the path toward greater emotional maturity and effectiveness.

NOT JUST AVOIDING THE NEGATIVES

Emotional maturity is about more than maintaining emotional control in challenging moments in order to avoid the damaging effects of unchecked negative emotion. It also means releasing and sharing emotions in healthy ways. "Healthy ways" doesn't mean that emotionally mature leaders never upset anyone. In fact, for leaders who have a significant fear of conflict, being emotionally mature means sharing their thoughts and feelings even if doing so upsets someone.

Emotional maturity means being aware of when you upset others—preferably knowing that it will upset others *before* you do it—and choosing to do so when wisdom whispers that it's the best course of action, all things considered. Emotional maturity is choosing when and how to encourage and admonish, as opposed to letting your emotions tell you when those things are going to happen. Inseparable from the concept of emotional maturity is the value of sincerely connecting with people and helping them do the same with you and each other.

Some leaders define emotional maturity in leadership as the leader playing the role of emotional puppet master. In this way of thinking, emotional maturity is seen as the leader consistently pushing just the right emotional buttons at just the right times to manipulate followers to do what the leader wants them to do with great enthusiasm. Leaders who see emotional maturity in this way miss the core of what emotional maturity is. They don't understand the value of actually becoming emotionally mature themselves. They don't see that emotional maturity is as much about leaders valuing genuine human connection and giving others their very best emotional selves as it is about managing their followers' emotions.

THE RISE AND FALL OF THE PHYSIOLOGICAL EFFECTS OF EMOTION TAKES SIX SECONDS. ONE SIMPLE METHOD FOR BECOMING MORE EMOTIONALLY MATURE IS FOR US TO SLOW DOWN WHEN WE ARE EMOTIONALLY TRIGGERED.

THE OIL REFINERY

For some leaders, there may appear to be a philosophical conflict between being emotionally mature and being authentic (the latter of which we discussed in Chapter 5 as part of being principled).

Does being measured, conscious, and intentional about how we share our emotions make us less real, less genuine, or less authentic? The answer is no. Let me explain.

Think about times when you've let your immediate, internal reactions to people or situations run unchecked. When you soberly step away from the moment of being triggered, would you say that your immediate, internal reaction accurately represented the full spectrum of emotions you had about the person or situation? In most instances, the answer is no. We usually have a greater range of emotions than our initial reactions display. True, we may have frustration or even rage that shows up immediately. But, if we ask ourselves a few "why?" questions, we often find more constructive emotions that connect to hope for the projects and people with whom we work. Thus, we find that our immediate, internal reactions have only masqueraded as our true emotions, making them less authentic than the measured and thoughtful emotions that we respond from when we are not in a triggered state.

The best analogy I've been taught to understand being emotionally mature while remaining authentic is that of an oil refinery.[8] When oil comes out of the ground, we refer to it as "crude oil" because that's exactly what it is—crude. It is unrefined and therefore limited in its value. However, after it has gone through the refining process, it becomes a variety of valuable products, one class of which is called "fuel oils." Jet fuel and diesel fall into this category. These fuel oils are valuable commodities that literally propel airplanes and machinery for productive uses. Whether entering or exiting the refinery, we accurately call the material "oil." But there is a world of difference between the value of what goes in and the value what comes out.

The oil refining process is analogous to being emotionally mature while simultaneously being authentic. We call what we feel "emotions," whether refined or not. But if we allow ourselves time—sometimes as little as six seconds—to process and refine our emotions, what comes out is significantly more valuable and more capable of propelling others toward productive purposes than the crude emotions of our immediate, internal reactions.

Pausing to refine our immediate, internal reactions not only makes our emotions more valuable, it also more accurately represents the breadth and depth of our emotions, thereby making us more authentic. There is no conflict between being emotionally mature and being authentic. In fact, they align with each other.

$2 BILLION AND PLAYING CATCH

One of my all-time favorite stories about being emotionally mature came from a senior executive of an international manufacturing company. In the midst of a *Who* Not What* journey with his leadership team, he shared that being more curious in combination with being more empathic had been helpful in the process of finalizing an opportunity worth more than $2 billion (USD). This deal was a step change for his company. I was, of course, pleased that our leadership development work had been helpful to him and the organization. But it was the next story he shared with me—a story about baseball and his relationship with his son—that really stuck with me about the power of emotional maturity in a leader. Here is that story in his own words.

> *"The most enlightening experience for me where I exercised greater emotional maturity involved my 12-year-old son and baseball.*

*3/4 OF YOUR EFFECTIVENESS AS A LEADER COMES FROM WHO YOU ARE, NOT WHAT YOU DO

"*I don't just like baseball. I love it. And I don't just follow a team. I live and die with the New York Yankees. I have since 1961. In that year, I had a brief flirtation with the 1960 Cincinnati Reds (Pete Rose's rookie year). But I recognized that the team my dad followed had in its center field a remarkable player who I could watch every week on local New York television, Mickey Mantle. In 1961 I watched as he and Roger Maris chased after Babe Ruth's 60 home run record right through to the World Series where they crushed the Reds in four games. After that, I was hooked on the Yankees for life.*

"*My passion for baseball led to decades of playing catch, first with my dad and older brother, and then with my eldest three sons. As my boys grew through the ages of 7 to 18, warm days in the spring found us taking out our baseball gloves and throwing popups or ground balls and striking out imaginary batters. We did so for hours and hours. In the process, they each got very good at ball handling, and we all shared an interest in baseball highlighted by yearly trips to Yankee Stadium to visit the house that Ruth built.*

"*My fourth son, however, never took to the game. Early efforts at Little League left him disinterested and unwilling to put in the time to get better. I had all but given up on him having an interest in the game when my wife informed me that he was going to go to a baseball camp for a week and that I needed to practice with him before he went. I dreaded a repeat of our many other sessions where, just as we seemed to get started, he wanted to do something different. This was usually followed by me trying to get him to stick to it over his protests. It usually ended poorly.*

"I was concerned about my absence from home (because of my job) so I decided to suck it up and try again to make something work. Just spending time with him was going to have to be enough. I resigned myself not to resist his efforts to dictate how and what we did. And wouldn't you know, after five years of fruitless effort, we had the best several weeks of extended ball catching that we have ever had. Instead of doing it in 1-hour and 2-hour stints, we did it in multiple 20-minute stints at his call. A couple of times in the morning and then in the afternoon and evening. When he wanted to move on, I didn't resist. I told him to get me when he wanted to do it again. That is how the vacation went. It may not sound like much, but I finally connected with him in a way I hadn't before. It was special.

"Being emotionally mature does involve putting the interests of others ahead of my own selfish interests and emotional desires. It required that I suspend my judgment about how things were to be done and accept what emotionally worked for him. I felt like an eyewitness to a spaceship landing. He got better and better. He caught popups, fastballs, ground balls, and his throwing improved dramatically. I could kick myself in the ass for not having hit on this sooner. Let him decide and let him set the pace. Quit being such a control freak and just go with the flow.

"It is difficult to comprehend that something I had hoped for and had given up on was so easily achieved by

*getting out of my own way and letting him run the show.
After all, he knew best what would work for him. And in
the process of him getting what he needed, I got a gift I'd
been waiting for—waiting for for years."*

Emotional maturity is a powerful thing—even more so in
the hands of a leader. When we as leaders are able to recognize
our desires and the emotions attached to them while fully seeing
the emotional realities and needs of others, increased energy,
connection, influence, and information are the result. Emotional
maturity benefits everyone involved, including the leader.

Our detailed investigation of what makes up a well-developed
Who is now complete. Next, we turn our attention to how it all
works together to create exceptional leadership results.

"The result of long-term relationships is better and better quality, and lower and lower costs."

W. EDWARDS DEMING

CHAPTER EIGHT

A Matter of Trust

EXPLORING THE CONNECTION BETWEEN
THE *WHO* OF LEADERSHIP AND PRODUCING RESULTS

Have you ever found yourself in a season of life in which you didn't trust your boss? Think back to the emails and phone calls during that season. How much extra time and effort went into communication? Do you remember editing emails repeatedly, trying to find the right tone so your leader would hear what you meant despite the tenuous relationship? Or maybe you found yourself scribbling notes after short hallway conversations because you believed you needed to protect yourself from how others might "remember" what they said. Maybe you've repeatedly hit the pound button on the phone after leaving a voicemail so you could re-record and re-record and re-record your message because you didn't trust that your tone and words would be taken as you intended. These common experiences in the workplace represent wasted time, energy, and money. Each is an inefficiency in organizational life. This is what a lack of trust in leadership gets us.

As a visual reminder of this principle, I have a stack of email correspondence about 40 pages long. It's an email discussion between Gerald, a district manager for a wholesale window distributor, and one of his direct reports, Jiahui. Gerald and Jiahui were locked in a conversation about compensation—specifically Jiahui's bonus. Jiahui was about to leave the company, and Gerald had promised Jiahui that if she were to talk openly with him about her potential departure, Jiahui's bonus would not be affected. Jiahui agreed. For several months they discussed the timing of Jiahui's departure, the transition of her responsibilities, and her bonus. Jiahui saved electronic and hard copies of every correspondence in order to protect herself because she didn't trust Gerald.

Those 40 pages in my office represent not only the time it took to write them in just the right way—carefully choosing words in order to say enough without saying too much—but also all of the emotional energy poured into the situation by Jiahui as she processed it with colleagues, her family, and by herself. Not a single word on those sheets of paper is about moving the mission of Gerald's team, the department, or the company forward. It's all sideways energy. This stack of paper tangibly reminds me that a lack of trust in leadership isn't just unpleasant; it's also painfully inefficient and financially expensive.

Imagine a world in which there were no extra emails and phone calls attributable to a lack of trust between followers and their leaders. How much time and energy would be saved? All of that time and energy could be re-directed toward the goals of the enterprise or team. With about 7.5 billion people on Earth, it is not a stretch to estimate that more than a billion hours per year are lost because of a lack of trust in leaders. Becoming a well-developed *Who* is not only more enjoyable to the follower, but it's also a more efficient way to lead. No wonder it produces better results.

TRUST, TRUST, AND MORE TRUST

One of the most fascinating discoveries I've come upon, is the difference between the level of trust inspired by leaders who are Inwardly Sound and Others Focused versus the level of trust achieved by leaders who are only Inwardly Sound. Vanessa Kiley, the researcher and consultant who originally crunched the numbers discussed in Chapter 3, pointed me to this discovery. She shared with me that maximum levels of trust—and therefore efficiency—can't be reached without the leader being Others Focused. Why is that? Consider the two levels of trust (Figure 11).

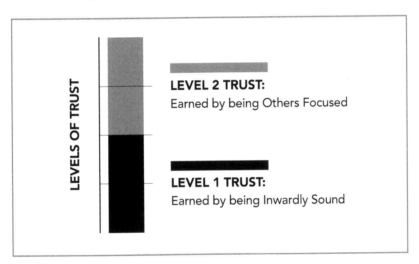

Figure 11: Trust Levels Leaders Earn from Their Followers

Level 1 Trust between leaders and followers is influenced by all aspects of being Inwardly Sound, with special emphasis on being principled. Level 2 Trust, on the other hand, is influenced by being Others Focused. Level 2 Trust takes the foundation of Level 1 Trust and builds on it by taking suspicion out of the relational equation for followers.

Leaders who are Inwardly Sound but *not* Others Focused leave the door open for followers to question their motives . . . and justifiably so. These leaders make themselves the primary beneficiaries of their leadership efforts. Some do it unconsciously, but that still undermines followers' trust. These leaders require their followers to be on alert, to be suspicious. Followers are invited to wonder if the direction they're being led is for the benefit of themselves, the leader, or the enterprise. Consequently, a portion of their enthusiastic followership is bridled.

> **LEADERS WHO ARE INWARDLY SOUND BUT NOT OTHERS FOCUSED LEAVE THE DOOR OPEN FOR FOLLOWERS TO QUESTION THEIR MOTIVES . . . AND JUSTIFIABLY SO.**

Then there are leaders who are Others Focused but not Inwardly Sound. I've never observed a leader who was Others Focused and blatantly lacked being principled. But I have seen leaders who worked to be Others Focused while lacking the other aspects of being Inwardly Sound. It diminished followers' ability to trust them because their lack of inner stability and development created havoc that negated and undermined their best efforts to be Others Focused.

We could go through each of the aspects of being an Inwardly Sound leader to identify how trust suffers when each is absent, but for now we'll focus on being self-aware. Has someone ever corrected you without seeing his or her own contribution to the negative situation? Have you ever seen a leader look everywhere but in the mirror for the solution to a problem? Do you trust such leaders? Probably not. We rarely trust leaders who lack self-awareness, regardless of their expertise. Emotionally, we just don't want to hear from the person who can't or isn't willing to see his or her own issues. Logically, we don't trust those leaders because when they can't see themselves accurately, they are under-informed and appear to be unwise.

Level 2 Trust can't be achieved without a foundation of Level 1 Trust—created by being Inwardly Sound—to build upon. Leaders who are both Inwardly Sound and Others Focused remove suspicion and restrictive levels of caution from the relational equation. In doing so, they create Level 2 Trust with their followers, which in turn produces more efficient relationships and communication.

Simon Sinek, famed TED talk deliverer and organizational consultant, says, "When we have to protect ourselves from each other, the whole organization suffers. But when trust and cooperation thrive internally, we pull together and the organization grows stronger as a result."[1] Trust is at the core of organizational effectiveness because of its profound impact on relational efficiency. Though I enjoy a good whitewater-rafting team-building trip as much as the next person, if our desire as leaders is to have efficient and effective relationships with those we lead, we should be less focused on building trust and more focused on being trustworthy. And that is achieved by being and becoming a little more Inwardly Sound and Others Focused every day.

A SURPRISING CONNECTION

The value of the trust created by being Inwardly Sound and Others Focused isn't limited to more efficient relationships and communication. It also has a surprising influence on motivation

*3/4 OF YOUR EFFECTIVENESS AS A LEADER COMES FROM WHO YOU ARE, NOT WHAT YOU DO

and engagement.

Challenges and encouragements from trustworthy leaders motivate us to action in ways that the same comments from leaders we don't trust can't. Why is that? The emotional roadblocks of suspicion and caution don't exist—or exist to a much lesser extent—with those we deeply trust. We allow our spirits to soar on encouragement and more fully embrace challenge from leaders we trust. Both result in greater energy, engagement, and motivation in followers.

WE SHOULD BE LESS FOCUSED ON BUILDING TRUST AND MORE FOCUSED ON BEING TRUSTWORTHY.

It's critical to remember the relationship between a leader's trustworthiness and a follower's motivation and engagement when evaluating performance and results. Little of value has ever been done without motivation and engagement. In fact, these two are often the great salve of strategic shortcomings in leadership. If two teams are racing from Point A to Point B, one on a straight path and one on a curved path, who will win? The answer: It depends on how fast the two teams are running. When our strategic choices aren't perfect (i.e., the curved path), we can still succeed as leaders if our followers are motivated and engaged to run fast.

To make it a little more personal and a little more obvious, I'd like to take you through one my favorite exercises to do with clients. It requires some visualization, so if you can, find a quiet place to sit.

First, I'd like you to write down the name of someone you really, really DON'T trust. (I don't find that people have difficulty coming up with this person's name. It usually pops to mind pretty quickly.) Pretend this person just sent you an email. Vividly imagine—this is the visualization piece—clicking on your email and then reading the following (Figure 12):

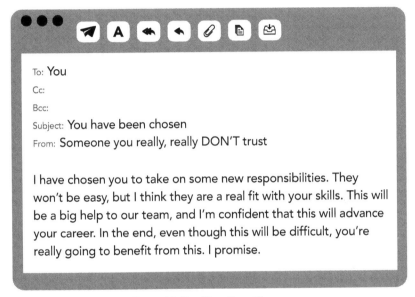

Figure 12: You Have Been Chosen

On a scale of 0 to 10, with 10 being coming-out-of-your-skin excited, and 0 being at the opposite end of the spectrum, write down how motivated and engaged you feel after receiving this message from the person you really, really DON'T trust (Figure 13).

Figure 13: How Motivated and Engaged are You?

Now we're going to try a different visualization. Take a moment to write the name of someone you really, really DO trust. Pretend this person has just sent you an email. Vividly imagine clicking on your email and then reading the following (Figure 14):

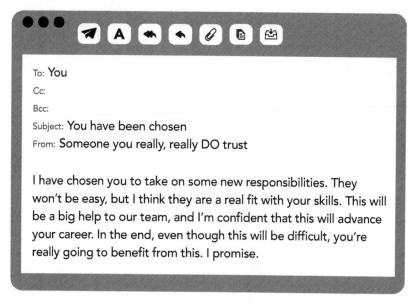

Figure 14: You Have Been Chosen—Round #2

On a scale of 0 to 10, with 10 being coming-out-of-your-skin excited, rate how motivated and engaged you feel after receiving this message from the person you really, really DO trust (Figure 15).

Figure 15: How Motivated and Engaged are You?—Round #2

So here's the question: Did you put down a bigger number for the person you trusted or the person you didn't trust? Of course the person you trusted received a higher number.

I've never had a person put a smaller number down—or even an equal number—for the person that is trusted versus the person who is not trusted. Every single person with whom I've ever done this exercise identifies themselves as more motivated and engaged about the opportunity described in the email when receiving it from someone they trust. But they're not just a little more motivated and engaged. They're *a lot more* motivated and engaged. I've started keeping track of the numeric difference between the untrusted person and the trusted person. On average, the numeric change in motivation and engagement is greater than 200%. That change is based on one thing and one thing alone: the trustworthiness of the person delivering the message. Trust is engaging.

I once heard the late Norman Schwarzkopf speak at a conference in St. Louis. The four-star general and former leader of the United States Central Command and Operation Desert Shield said, "Good people can make a bad plan work." Motivated and engaged people can do the same. It behooves us, then, to remember that being trustworthy as a leader supercharges the motivation and engagement of those who follow us.

While the connection between trust and engagement may be clear at this point, some may find themselves still suspicious of the connection between engagement and results. If that's you, I get it. My engineering background tends to want data to support ideas even if they seem logical. So is there a scientific study that proves that greater engagement leads to better results? Yes, there is. To be more specific, there are more than 300 such studies.

A Gallup meta study[2] of 339 different studies involving 230 companies, 49 industries, 73 countries, and over 1.8 million employees found that the companies in the top quartile of engagement versus companies in the bottom quartile of engagement had:

21% higher	profitability
20% higher	sales
17% higher	productivity
10% higher	customer metrics
59% lower	turnover in low-turnover organizations
24% lower	turnover in high-turnover organizations
28% lower	loss of inventory
70% fewer	safety incidents
41% lower	absenteeism
40% fewer	quality defects

When we pause to observe the interplay of the elements, a pattern emerges. We see a path that connects *Who* to performance and results. When leaders are more Inwardly Sound and Others Focused, they are more trustworthy. When they are more trustworthy, motivation and engagement increase. When motivation and engagement increase, results and performance rise. We call this series of causes and effects The Arc of Leadership (Figure 16). It is one thing to statistically identify that the *Who* * *Not What Principle* exists. It is another thing to understand why it exists. The Arc of Leadership shows us why the *Who* * *Not What Principle* exists.

COMPETITIVE ADVANTAGE

This all leads to a question: Is there actual opportunity for competitive advantage in the marketplace by increasing employee

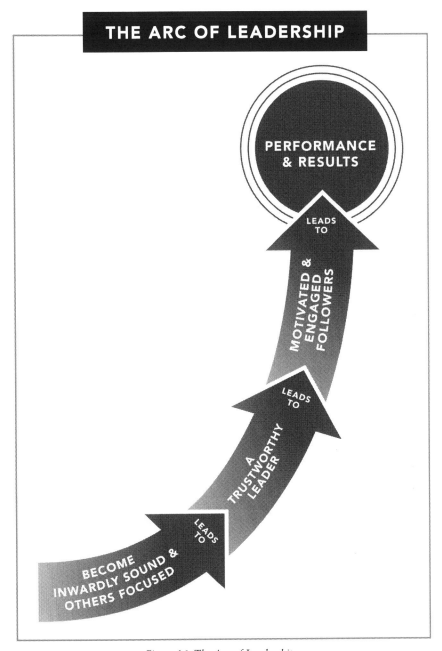

Figure 16: The Arc of Leadership

*3/4 OF YOUR EFFECTIVENESS AS A LEADER COMES FROM WHO YOU ARE, NOT WHAT YOU DO

engagement? The emphatic answer is "Yes!" Gallup calculates that just 15% of full-time employees worldwide are engaged in their work (Figure 17).[3] Developmental Dimensions International, Towers Watson, and The Corporate Executive Board have all produced similar findings.[4]

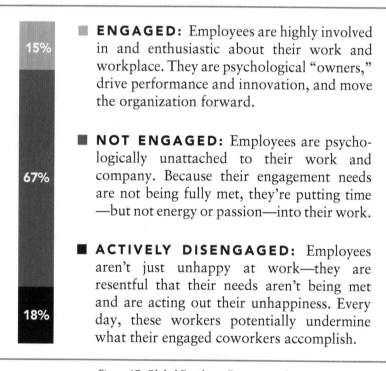

ENGAGED: Employees are highly involved in and enthusiastic about their work and workplace. They are psychological "owners," drive performance and innovation, and move the organization forward.

NOT ENGAGED: Employees are psychologically unattached to their work and company. Because their engagement needs are not being fully met, they're putting time —but not energy or passion—into their work.

ACTIVELY DISENGAGED: Employees aren't just unhappy at work—they are resentful that their needs aren't being met and are acting out their unhappiness. Every day, these workers potentially undermine what their engaged coworkers accomplish.

Figure 17: Global Employee Engagement [5]

The United States employee engagement level is 33%—more than double the worldwide mark. That sounds good until we do the math and realize that 67% of the US workforce is not engaged, with 16% of those surveyed falling into the actively disengaged category.[6] These anemic levels of employee engagement create tremendous opportunity for marketplace advantage.

Imagine what would happen if trustworthy leaders built a company where 70% of employees were engaged. We actually don't have to imagine. We have data. Winners of Gallup's Great Workplace Award found that, on average, 70% of their employees landed in the "engaged" category.[7] What did all that engagement produce? Publicly traded companies who won the award experienced an Earnings Per Share (EPS) growth of 115% compared to EPS growth of just 27% for their competitors.[8] Very simply, because of the relationship between *Who*, trust, engagement, and performance, it is strategically astute for individuals to become and for companies to develop trustworthy leaders.

The impact of high levels of trust can be seen in business data. An Interaction Associates study found that organizations with highly trusted leaders out performed organizations with poorly trusted leaders by 56% in customer loyalty and retention, 58% in competitive market positioning, and 95% in predictable business/financial results.[9] Great Place to Work®, the company that collects and crunches data for *Fortune* magazine's 100 Best Companies to Work For® issue, touts trust as a crucial component within companies that land on their

IT IS STRATEGICALLY ASTUTE FOR INDIVIDUALS TO BECOME AND FOR COMPANIES TO DEVELOP TRUSTWORTHY LEADERS.

top 100 list.[10] That group of companies has cumulative stock market returns nearly triple that of the general market since 1998.[11] Unless you believe that high-trust organizations can be built and maintained by leaders who are themselves untrustworthy, the connection between trustworthy leaders and measurable financial and business performance is unmistakable.

LEADERSHIP TEAM COHESION

Competitive advantage is not binary—it's a continuum wherein the more trustworthy leaders become, the more competitive advantage they experience. When leaders work together with their peers—as opposed to by themselves—to become more Inwardly Sound and Others Focused, they often find themselves pushed higher on that continuum.

More than one executive leader has shared with me how the dynamics within their leadership teams have improved as a result of their *Who* Not What* efforts. Even leaders who have already worked together for years have discovered a better understanding of each other and greater team cohesion by taking the *Who* Not What* journey together.

I confess that this outcome was not a goal or expectation of mine when I began supporting leadership teams in their *Who* Not What* development. At the time, I was solely focused on helping individual leaders maximize their potential. But, in retrospect, I should have seen it coming. It only makes sense that vulnerably exploring the personal qualities of *Who* side-by-side with peers over time would grow trust and connect leaders to one another in unique and helpful ways. Near the end of a multi-year journey into *Who* Not What*, one senior executive described it this way:

> *"Before Who* Not What, we worked more as a coalition of high-performing individuals rather than as a team. Now we are a high-performing team. Our Who**

Not What work built trust and gave us greater under-standing of who each of us are as people. This is the glue that keeps high-performing teams working together."

As leaders journey together in *Who* Not What*, two meaningful outcomes occur: (1) They become more Inwardly Sound and Others Focused, and (2) they get to know each other at a far more personal level. Because of these, trust soars. As a result, much of the energy that was previously used for infighting and politicking gets reallocated toward engaging in constructive conflict, resolving the organization's challenges, and strategically pursuing its opportunities. When you consider the time and energy often spent on politics and unhealthy relationships within leadership teams, the benefits of walking this developmental path with peers are a very real competitive advantage.

MEASURED BY MCKINSEY

Competitive advantages need not stop at deeper connections within leadership teams. If organizations are willing to develop the *Who* of their leaders at multiple levels of leadership through-out the company, organizational health is an additional com-petitive advantage that shows up. We have a globally-sourced measurement to help us see this in action.

One of my clients engaged McKinsey & Company[12] to calculate their organizational effectiveness shortly before they began their *Who* Not What* journey. McKinsey did so by using its Organizational Health Index (OHI). The OHI is known for its global benchmarking—over 5 million data points across 100 countries—and statistical connection to financial

*3/4 OF YOUR EFFECTIVENESS AS A LEADER COMES FROM WHO YOU ARE, NOT WHAT YOU DO

performance.[13]

The organization's leaders brought leadership development efforts rooted in the truth of *Who* Not What* to more than just their senior leadership team. They engaged over 100 of their middle managers and a select number of frontline leaders in *Who*-based leadership development. As this happened, over the course of five years, their OHI score rose from the bottom quartile (raw score of 59) to the top quartile (raw score of 72), globally. That's a 22% increase in OHI.

To be sure, *Who* Not What* was not the client's only improvement endeavor. They implemented a number of important changes upon learning they were in the bottom quartile of OHI ratings. But multiple senior leaders in the organization shared with me that their *Who* Not What* work played an important role in improving their organizational health. Said one of its leaders:

> *"When I think about the contribution of Who* Not What to the improvement in our OHI, I go to leadership. One of the clear components of OHI is leadership. I think it's a fact that we've developed a deep respect that everybody in the organization can contribute to our success. And I think that's been a fundamental change. Our people see that we value them. We're not there as a leadership team looking at them as objects of our ultimate performance or as pawns in a game. It's now a deep and genuine belief that they matter, their ideas matter, and they see that. I think that helped shift the dial on organizational health. Was that the only factor? No. But Who* Not What's influence was substantial."*

What results does organizational effectiveness like this produce? McKinsey calculates that companies in the top quartile of the OHI deliver, on average, three times greater returns to their shareholders and are more than twice as likely to have financial performance above the median than those in the bottom quartile.[14]

Here again we see a connection between becoming more well-developed *Whos* and competitive advantages that produce quantifiable results. The organization's top brass decided to engage a large number of their leaders in the inner development of who they are as people, and then reaped the rewards for doing so.

When, would you guess, is the first time you can really begin to develop others as leaders? When they receive their first leadership positions, right? Wrong.

As we think about trust and the realities of being a leader who is Inwardly Sound and Others Focused, an odd and un-expected truth pokes its head out of the ground. We see that much of the most critical work of becoming an exceptional leader happens in the inner recesses of the leader. The ironic reality of this is that we don't actually need followers to work on these things. You read that right. No followers are required to become more Inwardly Sound and Others Focused (which is 3/4 of leadership effectiveness). We can develop who we are—who we must become in order to maximize our potential

*3/4 OF YOUR EFFECTIVENESS AS A LEADER COMES FROM WHO YOU ARE, NOT WHAT YOU DO

as leaders—without followers because it's internal work within the leader.

This is great news for those leading aspiring leaders who have yet to acquire followers. You can help them begin a deep dive into the most powerful aspects of leadership before they have anyone to lead. In fact, one might argue it's better for them to do so without followers because they won't screw anyone up while getting their own houses in order.

And if you are one of those aspiring leaders without followers yet, congratulations! You can begin the most important leadership development of your life today without having a single follower.

WHO TRUSTS FIRST?

While becoming worthy of the trust of those we lead is essential to lead effectively, choosing to go first in trusting others is also important and directly fueled by being a well-developed *Who*.

Mike Kane, CEO and Managing Director of Boral Limited, says it is the responsibility of leaders to go first in the act of trusting. "It is first for leaders to trust followers, not for followers to first trust leaders. Leaders must lead—as in actually go first—in trusting others. Why? Because extending trust is a risk. You are asking too much of subordinates to ask them to step out on the bridge first. The risks are imbalanced. Leaders must demonstrate trust first if they want trust reciprocated. Leading with trust is the burden of the leader."

Some leaders struggle with this notion. They approach followers as if saying, "I will trust you only after you prove yourself worthy of that trust. Until then, I'm going to assume at all times that you are about to screw everything up." In doing so, these leaders display their need to become more Inwardly Sound. Yes, such leaders may have had followers let them down in the past. But vowing to start from a place of distrust of followers speaks more to the leader's unhealed wounding and unfinished work of becoming Inwardly Sound than to that of incapable followers.

There are two key qualities of *Who* that enable leaders to go first in the dance of who will trust the other first: leader or follower. Both qualities are part of being Inwardly Sound. The first and most foundational is that the leader be secure and set-tled. The leader's ability to not believe and act as if his or her future is on the line with every choice a follower makes enables the leader to extend trust to the follower more easily. The malady of self-protection is where a good deal of micromanagement in leadership is sourced. Even if the leader's future really is on the line—which happens far rarer than we believe it does—the perspective that all will be okay (being settled), even if the

IT IS FIRST FOR LEADERS TO TRUST FOLLOWERS, NOT FOR FOLLOWERS TO FIRST TRUST LEADERS. LEADERS MUST LEAD—AS IN ACTUALLY GO FIRST—IN TRUSTING OTHERS.

initiative or project goes belly up, allows the leader to risk trust-ing followers first.

In addition to being secure and settled, being courageous (part of being Inwardly Sound: Principled) also enables leaders to trust followers before those followers have extended trust to their leaders. This reality coincides with the risk that Mike Kane

*3/4 OF YOUR EFFECTIVENESS AS A LEADER COMES FROM WHO YOU ARE, NOT WHAT YOU DO

noted. Followers are almost always in a more precarious position than leaders due to the power imbalance between leaders and followers. Thus, it is riskier for them to trust first, necessitating leaders to go first. Even so, it is not without risk for the leader to trust first. The leader must be courageous.

To encourage leaders to go first in trusting, consider that the natural reaction of followers who are trusted is rarely to abuse that trust. Rather, they are almost always inspired to attempt to rise to the occasion and are often successful in doing so. I observed a rich example of this a few years ago.

DOLLHOUSE TRUST

A group of us had gathered to lend a hand to our friends, Matt and Meredith, who were moving. In the midst of loading and unloading, Meredith pulled aside my friend, Francisco, and made a special request related to her two-year-old daughter's prized possession. She said, "Francisco, I trust you to move this dollhouse. I don't trust those other guys. But you, I trust."

He told me that he has never moved a piece of furniture so carefully in his life.

Meredith had chosen him. Meredith had trusted him. And it played on something deep within him. She didn't hover over him or try to control the situation. She simply chose him, trusted him, and told him she was doing so.

New York Times and *Wall Street Journal* bestselling author Dan Pink calls this element of motivation "autonomy." In his classic work on motivational factors, American psychologist Fredrick Herzberg explained it as knowing that our decisions make a difference. No matter how you articulate it, it is deeply motivating (and satisfying!) to be given the responsibility for something meaningful and the authority to make it happen—being trusted. It creates ownership that fuels a sense of purpose, follow through, care, and commitment. In short, it unleashes motivation.

Imagine if Meredith had instead announced, "Okay! I need someone to move this dollhouse. Anyone will do, because I've got a detailed plan for how you're going to do it. Oh, and I'll be nearby at all times, you know, just to make sure everything goes okay."

Slightly less inspiring.

Yet at times, we as leaders are tempted to not trust. We try to manage the detailed actions of someone to achieve a particular end result. Even with the best intentions, that doesn't create ownership for others. It doesn't inspire purpose, follow through, care, or commitment within our followers. It doesn't unleash motivation.

When we extend trust to those we lead first, we create ownership and motivation within them. That's exactly what Meredith did for Francisco. She tapped into a core human motivation by trusting him to do something that mattered. That dollhouse made it to her daughter's new bedroom as pristine as it was in her old bedroom. Francisco accomplished that. And he was proud of it—not only for having done it, but also because Meredith had trusted him to do it. And on top of the job getting done, their friendship took a step forward as well.

To be sure, there are many factors that go into a follower doing a job well. But one of the first steps in that process is the leader being Inwardly Sound enough to trust first.

ACTUALLY BECOMING

We can't finish this part of the book without discussing further the idea of *becoming*. Though becoming a leader who is Inwardly Sound and Others Focused is hard work, it is actually more efficient than constantly trying to create the perception that we're Inwardly Sound and Others Focused. Let me explain.

When initially confronted with the truth of *Who* Not What,* many people (myself included) begin their leader-development efforts by asking themselves questions like, "What would a humble leader do in this situation?" or, "How would an emotionally mature leader act under these circumstances?" These aren't bad questions per se. Answering them begins to reveal the direction we need to go. But if we don't commit ourselves to actually becoming humble and emotionally mature, we'll find ourselves asking those same questions over and over again for the rest of our leadership lives.

If you have 30 years left in your career of leading, imagine spending every day saying to yourself, "In each interaction today, I have to behave in such a way that the people I lead will believe I am Inwardly Sound and Others Focused even if I'm not." Doesn't having to manage everybody's perception of you every day for the next 30 years sound like an exhausting way to live?

LEADERS MUST COMMIT THEMSELVES TO *ACTUALLY BECOMING* MORE WELL-DEVELOPED *WHOS.*

Compare that to doing the hard work of becoming more humble and emotionally mature. What if, instead of asking ourselves what humble and emotionally mature leaders would do, we asked ourselves, "Am I being humble?" or, "Am I being emotionally mature?"

Sure, the front side of *becoming* is more challenging than

merely shooting for perception management. But when the work is done, with maintenance and check-ins along the way, leaders can let their natural selves do the talking.

In the long run, becoming Inwardly Sound and Others Focused is more efficient in producing effective leadership than daily managing perception to act Inwardly Sound and Others Focused. And one more point: People know a fake when they see one—especially a fake leader they're following over the long haul. If we *become*, we don't have to fear being found out as a fake.

DEAL WITH IT

When we look at being Inwardly Sound and Others Focused, we find some of the very best humanity has to offer. But if we look at the antithesis of Inwardly Sound and Others Focused, we end up with insecure, untrustworthy, unhealthy, tentative, proud, greedy, emotionally immature, unloving leaders who lack self-awareness. Wow. What would it be like to follow those leaders? *Who* Not What* is alive and well in *all* leadership, both good and bad.

If we can be honest with ourselves, the antithesis of being Inwardly Sound and Others Focused lives in varying degrees within each of us. Few, if any, leaders are hindered by all the negative qualities listed in the previous paragraph. But who amongst us could say we wrestle with none of those issues? We all have things to work on if we are willing to look honestly at ourselves. And if we don't consciously work on the flaws within us, we'll be like most leaders—saddling our followers with the burden of having to figure out how to endure following us. In other words, if we don't deal with our own crap, our followers will have to.

---

*3/4 OF YOUR EFFECTIVENESS AS A LEADER COMES FROM WHO YOU ARE, NOT WHAT YOU DO

NOT JUST A BETTER WAY TO LEAD

Becoming Inwardly Sound and Others Focused has benefits beyond the experiences it creates for followers, the goals it achieves for enterprises, and the professional opportunities it produces for leaders. These additional benefits exist outside the realm of accomplishments and achievements. They live deep within leaders who choose to become Inwardly Sound and Others Focused.

The more Inwardly Sound we become, the more life seems to slow down. The fog of busyness and conflicting priorities that many experience as "normal life" thins for Inwardly Sound leaders. They have a rare clarity about life. Difficult choices are easier for them to make. They are less anxious. The stability within Inwardly Sound leaders benefits not only those they lead, but also themselves.

Leaders who are Others Focused experience an inner fulfillment that only generosity produces. Perhaps you've felt such gratification as you put together a Christmas present for a child. Or maybe you've mentored someone with no expectation of a return for yourself. If you've had such moments, you know the satisfaction that is birthed by truly selfless giving.

Leaders who choose to go down the developmental path of becoming more Inwardly Sound and Others Focused experience soulful benefits that exist on top of the external results that great leadership produces. These benefits sound like the cherry on top—a bonus we stumble upon as we become better leaders. But the truth is, they're one of the most valuable rewards of becoming a well-developed leader.

I was once coaching a teachable leader named Alice. She had been through a rough patch in her career and was taking stock of what to do next. As our discussions progressed, she started to investigate in detail the idea of being Others Focused. She began to intentionally shift her focus from herself to those around her. As she did, her spouse commented that he was seeing a tangible and positive difference in her. In a subsequent conversation, I listed for Alice many of the beneficial outcomes of being a leader who is Others Focused. I finished by saying that being Others Focused "really is a better way to lead." Alice profoundly replied, "It's a better way to live."

Though initially aimed at being Others Focused alone, I believe Alice's words apply even more to being Inwardly Sound and Others Focused in combination. As we become more Inwardly Sound and Others Focused, we become more well-developed leaders. We produce better results through efficiencies and energy fueled by trust. Becoming Inwardly Sound and Others Focused is, in fact, a better way to lead. But it's more than that. It's a pathway to inner stability and deep satisfaction. Becoming a well-developed *Who* is not just a better way to lead—it's a better way to live.

BECOMING A WELL-DEVELOPED *WHO* IS NOT JUST A BETTER WAY TO LEAD—IT'S A BETTER WAY TO LIVE.

Though we've worked hard to define *Who** Not *What*, understand its influence on leadership, and see its connections to trust and results, we haven't eliminated all possibilities for misunderstanding it. In the next chapter, we'll take a crack at doing just that.

*3/4 OF YOUR EFFECTIVENESS AS A LEADER COMES FROM WHO YOU ARE, NOT WHAT YOU DO

"There is nothing clever about confusion."
WILLIAM WYLER

CHAPTER NINE

Myths and Misunderstandings

SETTING THE RECORD STRAIGHT ABOUT WHAT
WHO* NOT WHAT SAYS AND WHAT IT DOESN'T

It's possible to learn about *Who* Not What*, see the truth contained within it, and come to some less-than-accurate conclusions about it. Over time, I've kept track of the questions most often asked and the ideas most likely to be misunderstood about *Who* Not What*. Let's address them one by one.

MYTHS AND MISUNDERSTANDINGS #1

"There's no point in trying to become a more well-developed person because adults can't change. Who we are is pretty well decided by the time we reach our mid-20's. Working to become a more well-developed *Who* in order to be a more effective leader is a waste of time, money, and energy."

Many people hold the belief that the development of who we are as people is completed by our mid-20's. This perspective seems to have emerged from the work of Swiss psychologist, Jean Piaget. Piaget found that, compared to the rest of life, childhood and adolescence hold within them the greatest potential for cognitive growth and development.[1] While this is true, a lack of openness to change seen in some adults has caused many people to take Piaget's concepts too far. They erroneously conclude that meaningful growth cannot happen in adulthood. In fact, adults can grow and develop in significant ways. There is both scientific and anecdotal evidence to prove it.

As mentioned back in Chapter 5,[2] researchers Cheryl Armon and Theo Dawson found that moral development does occur later in life.[3] Starting with Lawrence Kohlberg's theory and research in the stage development of moral reasoning,[4] Armon and Dawson interviewed their subjects once every four years over a 13-year period. They found that moral development occurred in all ages, including multiple adults who were more than 55 years old when the study began.

Additionally, Armon and Dawson found that not a single participant in their study reached the highest level of moral development—called "post-conventional reasoning"—before the age of 35. This aligned with a number of other studies noted by Armon and Dawson which showed that the highest levels of moral reasoning all occurred in adulthood.[5] This implies that not only can we develop the core of who we are later in life, but that a certain volume of life experiences is required if we are to reach the highest levels of moral development. (Of course, this is not to suggest that all or even most adults become fully developed morally. Simply having a 40th or 50th birthday does not automatically make anyone mature and morally sound.) The point here is that scientifically speaking, deep, inner development is possible for adults.

But does this research align with what we observe anecdotally in life? Let's answer this by asking a simple question. If you're over the age of 30 (assuming we reach "adulthood" by our mid-20's), look back on the last 5 years of your life. Would you say that you are exactly the same person today as you were 5 years ago? In all of my years of working with leaders—the vast majority of whom are decades past the age of 30—I've not once encountered a person who said they had not changed over the previous 5 years. Each of them felt that they had grown and developed. (Of course, by how much, compared to what those who follow them might have wished for, is another discussion.)

For further evidence, recall the McKinsey data gathered about one of my clients.[6] A group of the most senior leaders in that organization declared without request or provocation that the leadership development they had invested in had a material impact on their movement from the bottom quartile to the top quartile on McKinsey's OHI over the course of 5 years. And on whom was that leadership development focused? More than 80% of those involved were over the age of 30, with many over the age of 40 and some older than 50. And 100% of that work was aimed at helping those leaders become more well-developed in who they were as human beings—also known as becoming more Inwardly Sound and Others Focused. Even in client data, we see that adults *can* grow and develop in the inner core of who they are.

Finally, there is the example of Kelsey. In her early 40's, Kelsey is the CFO of a multi-national with whom I had the pleasure of working with for a number of years. Our work with Kelsey's organization was exclusively focused on the *Who* of Kelsey and each of her executive peers. About a year and a half into the engagement, Kelsey shared this with me.

*3/4 OF YOUR EFFECTIVENESS AS A LEADER COMES FROM WHO YOU ARE, NOT WHAT YOU DO

"I had a member of my team come to me recently and say, 'Eighteen months ago I was ready to leave the company and it was because of you. Now, I don't want to leave the company and it's because of you.' "

Kelsey had made such strides in developing who she was as a person, that someone in her charge had a 180-degree change in her perspective on following Kelsey. That shift was driven by Kelsey's willingness to work in developing the core of who she was, and Kelsey achieved that shift despite being well into adulthood.

In spite of the popular notion to the contrary, people *can* grow and develop in their adult years. The progress may not be as fast and obvious as it can be during childhood and adolescence, but due to the increased social and organizational influence leaders often enjoy later in life, the impact of their growth can be both profound and far reaching. To not invest in the development of *Who* you are, or *Who* others can become, due to an inaccurate belief that adults are not capable of meaningful change, is to miss out on one of the most valuable endeavors you can take on as a leader.

MYTHS AND MISUNDERSTANDINGS #2

"Who* Not What is about being a nice person.
Be a nice person and you'll be a good leader."

Being "nice" isn't nearly sufficient to describe a well-developed person and leader. Becoming Inwardly Sound and Others Focused is far more difficult and complex than becoming a nicer person.

Let's look at a couple of examples to debunk the idea that being a well-developed *Who* is about being nice.

First, let's clarify what we mean by the term "nice." A nice person is someone who is pleasant to be around. They get along with nearly everyone. They rarely, if ever, engage in difficult conflict.

There are times when we need our leaders to fight for what they see as best. We need them to be willing to initiate and instigate difficult conversations. We need them to engage in healthy conflict. In order to do this, we need them to be authentic and courageous—both hallmarks of being Inwardly Sound—even when it isn't convenient to do so.

People who "stir the pot" in this way aren't usually referred to as "nice." They may be referred to as "annoying" or "confrontational," but not "nice." Authentic and courageous leaders are well-developed people whose inner constitution exceeds the bounds of simply being nice.

For a second example of how "nice" is grossly insufficient to describe a well-developed *Who*, consider leaders who are insecure. These leaders spend an enormous chunk of their energy—not to mention the energy of those they lead—trying consciously and unconsciously to justify their existences. They sometimes protect turf and information in order to do so. They regularly make decisions fueled by the fear that they'll be found out as inadequate in their roles.

I once watched the president of an organization send her department heads out the door of a meeting with orders to come back with an analysis of what their departments would be able to contribute to a new, company-wide initiative. I was in the room when the head of the health and safety department gathered his

*3/4 OF YOUR EFFECTIVENESS AS A LEADER COMES FROM WHO YOU ARE, NOT WHAT YOU DO

team together. He accurately explained to the team what the initiative was all about. He then began the analysis by asking his team, "What do you think the president wants to hear from us?" He wasn't leading his team to analytically calculate what they would be able to contribute to the initiative. Instead, out of his deep insecurity, he led his team to come up with an answer he thought the president would like to hear. He didn't feel secure or confident enough to even entertain the possibility of bringing back an accurate answer that might be different than what the president hoped to hear. In short, he was leading poorly because he was leading out of his insecurity. And here's the kicker: This unhealthy, insecure, and ineffective leader is one of the nicest people I've ever met.

Being nice doesn't rid leaders of their insecurities. In fact, sometimes they are nice because they are insecure and deeply concerned with what others think about them. In that, their niceness is actually the symptom of a grave leadership liability.

Being a nice person is not the same as being a well-developed *Who*. It's possible to be both nice and underdeveloped at the same time. Maximizing your leadership potential by becoming a well-developed *Who* is about far more than being nice.

MYTHS AND MISUNDERSTANDINGS #3

"So what you're saying is all I have to do is be Inwardly Sound and Others Focused, and I'll be an exceptional leader. Nothing else matters."

No, that's not what *Who* Not *What* says. *Who* Not *What* speaks to the foundation of exceptional leadership. As seen through The Leadership Tree, *Who* is the currency that makes leadership activities such as execution, strategy creation, motivation, talent development, and vision clarity as valuable as they can be. But just as the foundation does not account for 100% of a building, *Who* does not account for everything it takes for leaders to reach their potential.

Imagine someone who was Inwardly Sound and Others Focused but was also inept in each aspect of the *What* of leadership. He or she would lack the ability to pursue vision, think strategically, marshal resources, ensure execution, unleash motivation, cultivate talent, drive culture, and communicate effectively. Would you want to follow an Inwardly Sound and Others Focused leader who lacked all of those abilities? Me neither. The truth is, we want and need our leaders to understand and apply the *What* of leadership while also being Inwardly Sound and Others Focused.

The *What* of leadership may not make up 3/4 of leadership as *Who* does, but the components of *What* are vitally important aspects of leadership that deserve attention and intention. Each has extensive and important concepts behind their titles. We won't do a deep dive into the *What* of leadership here. That's not because I'm not interested in the *What*—I am. Despite my passion for *Who* * Not *What*, I enjoy working with all areas of leadership. But to cover those details now would distract us from the focus of this book. For the time being, the titles for the *What* of leadership are clear enough to inform us what they are about. We'll leave detailed investigations of them for another time.

Who * Not *What* doesn't say the only thing that matters about leadership is *Who*. It identifies *Who* as the foundation on which the rest of the leader's abilities are built. *Who* is the most

---

*3/4 OF YOUR EFFECTIVENESS AS A LEADER COMES FROM WHO YOU ARE, NOT WHAT YOU DO

important factor in reaching our potential as leaders, but it isn't the *only* factor.

MYTHS AND MISUNDERSTANDINGS #4

"What about leaders who are successful but don't appear to be Inwardly Sound and Others Focused? Doesn't their existence prove that *Who* Not What* is false or at least not universally true?"

Though they don't come along frequently, there are leaders who are very successful without being Inwardly Sound and Others Focused. But their existence does not disprove *Who* Not What* as a principle. To make that point, let's look at a famous leader who fits the bill . . . or at least did until the latter part of his life.

Steve Jobs was a legendary innovator and visionary at Apple. He was, by many accounts, a tyrant. In his initial term as Apple's leader, his drive for progress seemed to outweigh nearly all of the humanity he could have shared with those he led. Said one of Jobs's biographers, Walter Isaacson: "He was not the world's greatest manager. In fact, he could have been one of the world's worst managers."[7]

When we see leaders who produce great results while having deficiencies in being Inwardly Sound and Others Focused, we can conclude they carry much larger buckets of capability in the *What* of leadership than most leaders. Their *What*, or aspects of their *What*, are so exceptional that they produce significant results without being Inwardly Sound and Others Focused. This was certainly the case with Jobs's ability to innovate and his vision for intuitively designed products. (The former is a core component in the *What* category of Think Strategically; the latter is a clear example of the *What* category of Pursue Vision.)

The important question in these cases isn't whether or not *Who* Not What* is true, but whether or not the leaders in question are reaching their full leadership potential. How much more effective would these leaders be if they were well-developed people—Inwardly Sound and Others Focused? What kind of leadership success would we see if a well-developed *Who* could be combined with the larger-than-normal *What* capabilities of these leaders?

To put a more specific face on those questions, what would have happened had Steve Jobs, for the whole of his life, combined his strategic ability to innovate with a greater consideration for how he impacted the lives of those he led? What might have been had his foresight into consumer-centric design been combined with empathy for those who were helping him develop Apple's products? While we can never fully know the answer to that question, we do have a very good clue that comes from Jobs himself.

In the biography entitled *Becoming Steve Jobs* by Brent Schlender and Rick Tetzeli, it is reported that Jobs became a far more well-developed person after his first term as Apple's leader. Schlender and Tetzeli make the case that it was Jobs's evolution as a person while at NeXT and Pixar—not his raw genius, which was already in play during his initial run with Apple—that enabled Apple's historic performance during his second tenure as its leader.[8] In this, we get to see in a single person the leadership effectiveness of both the genius who is underdeveloped as a person and the genius who has evolved to become a more well-developed human being. The first ended in significant personal financial gain for Jobs and the cold reality of being ousted from

*3/4 OF YOUR EFFECTIVENESS AS A LEADER COMES FROM WHO YOU ARE, NOT WHAT YOU DO

his own startup, while the latter produced nearly unimaginable personal wealth for Jobs and helped make Apple one of the most recognized, beloved, and valuable companies in the world.

When leaders are successful without being well-developed people, they aren't exceptions to the *Who* Not What Principle*. Instead, they are examples of success and unrealized leadership potential coexisting. In such circumstances, we need to acknowledge that, in spite of their achievements and exceptional *What* capabilities, these people could have had even greater effectiveness as leaders if they had successfully taken the journey of becoming more well-developed *Whos*.

MYTHS AND MISUNDERSTANDINGS #5

"If I work for a well-developed leader as described by Who* Not What, I'll be following a softie, kumbaya-type leader who is a strategic idiot."

If you find leaders who fit the softie, kumbaya-type, strategic idiot mold, you've encountered someone who has neglected the *What* of leadership and likely has a significant misunderstanding of leadership. Such leaders often take the form of an "over-relationer."

Over-relationers define leading well as being surrounded by warm relationships. They invest all of their time and effort in developing and maintaining positive but often thin relationships. They erroneously tell themselves and others that chummy relationships solve every leadership challenge. They define great leadership based on the momentary happiness of the people around them, neglecting the development of all other leadership qualities, including strategic thinking.

Because of their numerous positive relationships, such leaders might appear to be well developed on the surface. But a closer look often reveals that they aren't. Like a piece of fruit that looks great on the outside but is sour when you bite into it, these leaders are unhealthy internally. They've avoided their own inner work, most often in the arena of being Inwardly Sound. These over-relationers have come to their erroneous definition of excellent leadership by spending a lifetime leaning into their debilitating fear of conflict, excessive need for approval, or other similar inner maladies. They aren't the well-developed people and leaders they appear to be. Their warm relationships cover this up.

While the truth of *Who* Not What* does challenge leaders to put an extremely high priority on becoming Inwardly Sound and Others Focused, it doesn't ask them to do so at the exclusion of developing other leadership capabilities such as strategic thinking. If you find a softie, kumbaya-type, strategic-idiot leader, you've run into someone who has an understanding of leadership that will limit his or her effectiveness and who is likely not as well developed internally as he or she appears to be.

MYTHS AND MISUNDERSTANDINGS #6

"I've seen leaders who are not Inwardly Sound and Others Focused repeatedly get promoted up the chain of command in my organization. I've even seen them rewarded for violating the principles of being Inwardly Sound and Others Focused. If that's happening, how can *Who* Not What* be true?"

There's a fundamental difference between being promoted within a particular company and becoming an exceptional leader. They aren't one and the same. The fact is, the best leaders don't always

*3/4 OF YOUR EFFECTIVENESS AS A LEADER COMES FROM WHO YOU ARE, NOT WHAT YOU DO

get promoted. We might wish they did, but they don't. Why? Any number of factors, political and otherwise, can play out in organizations to promote less effective leaders over their more effective counterparts. In fact, this often happens because those making promotion decisions don't have a full understanding of how leadership actually works. The truth about leadership is hidden to them. When those making promotion decisions don't look deeply enough into the sources of leadership success and failure, they make promotion decisions based on the wrong criteria. In doing so, they put a governor on the potential success of their organizations.

Choosing to become a leader who is Inwardly Sound and Others Focused isn't a guarantee for promotion in any organization or industry. Your chance of promotion goes up significantly if you're an exceptional leader, but promotion is not guaranteed. For this reason, it's important that leaders who aspire to reach their potential honestly evaluate their motives for wanting to do so.

If you're someone who cares about reaching your leadership potential, I need to ask you a very important question:

> Do you want to reach your potential as a leader
> regardless of the professional opportunities that may
> or may not come along as a result of your leadership excellence?

I hope the answer is a strong "Yes." Those who answer "No" are attempting to use leadership for their own purposes, which, by definition, isn't Others Focused. These leaders are people acting the role of the exceptional leader in order to acquire the perks of sitting in the leader's chair or to help themselves feel good about who they are. Such individuals won't reach their potential as leaders. Those who follow them will sense their self-interest. Over time, followers can smell this type of manipulation all over their leaders.

None of this is to suggest that leaders should stay in organizations that don't understand leadership well in order to prove they want to be exceptional leaders for the right reasons. Our world doesn't become a better, more efficient place by letting underdeveloped leaders or organizational cultures emotionally beat down high-potential leaders. If you work in an organization that doesn't understand, value, and reward exceptional leadership—and you aspire to be a great leader—you should pause to consider if staying there is the best decision.

We must become leaders who are Inwardly Sound and Others Focused first and foremost for the value it creates for our followers and the enterprises in which we lead. These may be the only rewards we ever personally see if we're following leaders or working in organizations that don't understand the true foundation of exceptional leadership. Promotion and advancement are not guaranteed for exceptional leaders because getting promoted and being an exceptional leader are not the same thing.

MYTHS AND MISUNDERSTANDINGS #7

"Who* Not What may be true today,
but it sure wasn't 30 or 40 years ago."

Before we address this one, let's remember the difference between a trend and a principle. A trend is currently popular, though it wasn't so in the past and won't necessarily be so in the future. A principle has always been true and will always be so.

*3/4 OF YOUR EFFECTIVENESS AS A LEADER COMES FROM WHO YOU ARE, NOT WHAT YOU DO

Many Baby Boomers grow weary of the cultural, economic, business, demographic, and technology trends that enable younger generations to demand more from their workplaces and leaders. I've often heard complaints and negative character-izations about Gen Xers and Millennials from their Baby Boomer leaders. It isn't hard to understand why these Baby Boomers feel as they do. When growing up in the workforce, Baby Boomers didn't have nearly the same options—such as internet-based tools that allow young people to start and market new businesses from their dorm rooms.

Also, because of the population boom, those leading America's Baby Boom generation didn't have to be exceptional leaders to keep talented Baby Boomers. So many Boomers were available for each job that leaders' feet weren't held to the fire. If followers didn't like the way the leader led, they were invited to move on. There were plenty of competitive Baby Boomer peers willing to step in and take the job as it was. Additionally, Baby Boomers are the sons and daughters of those who lived through the Great Depression. Though they don't value steady employment as significantly as their parents, Baby Boomers value it significantly more than the generations that have come after them. This also influenced what type of leaders and the kind of work conditions Baby Boomers were willing to put up with.

None of this is meant to suggest there weren't great leaders in both the Silent (pre-Baby Boomer) or Baby Boomer generations. There were. I'm just acknowledging the environmental factors of the age. Baby Boomers began their careers at a time when demo-graphic and cultural factors conspired to ensure that leadership styles that are less effective over the long haul (e.g., autocratic leadership) were tolerated and in some cases even celebrated.

This all points out one very important sidebar: There's a difference between a leadership principle and the environment in which that principle is applied. This is an important concept for leaders to grasp. The factors of any particular environment—be they demographic conditions or organizational culture or current life cycle of the company or sophistication of the department or ethnic diversity of the project team or a million other contributors to the environments in which we lead—don't define what great leadership is or how it works. They only define the context in which we lead. It's a meta skill of leaders to be able to distinguish the contexts in which they lead from the leadership principles they espouse. If we are to lead well, we must be diligent about separating leadership principles from their applications so we can learn how to customize our applications of leadership principles (see The Leadership Tree—Figure 6 page 57) to best fit the environments in which we lead. But I digress. Let's return to the issue of the Baby Boomer environment.

When we look back on the time when Baby Boomers were entering and growing up in the workforce, the principle of *Who* Not What* was as alive and well then as it is today. Becoming a well-developed *Who* is difficult. So it's no surprise that in an age that didn't absolutely require it, Baby Boomers found themselves in environments that were tolerant of less-effective leadership and organizations.

> **IT'S A META SKILL OF LEADERS TO BE ABLE TO DISTINGUISH THE CONTEXTS IN WHICH THEY LEAD FROM THE LEADERSHIP PRINCIPLES THEY ESPOUSE.**

*3/4 OF YOUR EFFECTIVENESS AS A LEADER COMES FROM WHO YOU ARE, NOT WHAT YOU DO

While world economics and technological advancements are constantly changing, the foundation of exceptional leadership isn't. *Who* Not What* has always been true. If given the choice, we have and always will want to follow leaders who are Inwardly Sound and Others Focused. They are the most compelling leaders to follow.

The easiest way to determine if *Who* Not What* was true 30 or 40 years ago is to list the characteristics of being Inwardly Sound and Others Focused. Then ask Baby Boomers if, all other things being equal, they'd rather follow leaders with or without these qualities. The answer will be "with" every time. *Who* Not What* was as true 30 or 40 years ago as it is today. (And it always will be.)

MYTHS AND MISUNDERSTANDINGS #8

"Being Others Focused is about being customer-centric."

No, being Others Focused isn't about being customer-centric. Leaders who make this assumption take a more comfortable leadership path and miss the fundamental and most important aspects of what it means to be a leader who is Others Focused.

A friend and consultant, Steven Wilson, once challenged me to consider changing Others Focused to "Outwardly Focused." After all, doesn't being Others Focused require one to look outward? And isn't "Outwardly Focused" a mnemonically stickier yang to the ying of "Inwardly Sound"? To both questions I answered, "Yes." But I didn't make the change. Though such a shift may seem small, it is actually enormous when closely examined.

Making that change in terminology would invite leaders to miss the very personal nature of being Others Focused. This detrimental shift is something some leaders do already, even without calling it "Outwardly Focused." Some leaders interpret being Others Focused to mean paying closer attention to the needs of their customers as opposed to the internal needs of the organization. While this is often a smart business strategy, it is an erroneous interpretation of what it means to be Others Focused.

When leaders turn being Others Focused into the "Outwardly Focused" strategic exercise of listening well to their customers, they miss the importance of personally caring for and serving the people they lead. They exchange something intimate for something corporate. They move the essence of being Others Focused away from the relationships they have with those around them and toward organizational strategy. When they do this, they let themselves off the hook by pursuing a leadership path that requires less of their hearts and, consequently, means less to the people following them.

To define being Others Focused as being customer-centric is to misunderstand from where its power comes: the relationships you have with those you lead. Avoid this pitfall and you'll avoid losing the value and results that come from being Others Focused.

MYTHS AND MISUNDERSTANDINGS #9

"If a leader isn't Inwardly Sound and Others Focused, that leader is a bad person."

Learning about the truth of Who* Not What is both helpful and an invitation to judge our leaders. We should be careful about

*3/4 OF YOUR EFFECTIVENESS AS A LEADER COMES FROM WHO YOU ARE, NOT WHAT YOU DO

how far we take this judgment. If a leader hasn't done the work of becoming Inwardly Sound and Others Focused, that leader has unrealized potential. But that doesn't make him or her a bad person.

Human beings have a strong tendency to put people in all-or-nothing buckets. We see a single indiscretion or inconsiderate act and label the person a "bad apple" or worse. What would be funny—if it weren't so painfully true—is that we do just the opposite when we evaluate ourselves. When we make poor decisions, whether intentional or by accident, we give ourselves the benefit of the doubt.[9] We tell ourselves, "I was just having a bad day." Or we focus on the other times in life when we handled similar circumstances well. "That's not really me," we say. And on we go with the day.

There are plenty of good people and budding leaders with loads of potential who have not yet started down the intentional and challenging path of becoming Inwardly Sound and Others Focused. Think back to what lives in these two areas of leadership. They aren't light or simple characteristics to pursue. It's no wonder few do it well.

It's understandable that as the reality of *Who* * *Not* *What* confronts us, we evaluate our leaders and wish they were more Inwardly Sound and Others Focused. But let's be careful not to go too far with our judgments of them. They have "come by it honestly."[10] Most of them have been unconsciously formed by their experiences from birth until present day. That's not to say we should pretend that unhealthy and ineffective leaders are otherwise. But we can be less judgmental than we're tempted to be.

To have a "But for the grace of God go I" attitude and to give our leaders compassion and empathy as the truth of *Who* Not What* comes to rest in us, is to lean into our own development as leaders. It's a way of practicing one of the most critical leadership qualities: being humble.

MYTHS AND MISUNDERSTANDINGS #10

"You talk about insecurities being bad—as if people should eliminate all of their insecurities in order to be great leaders. But don't insecurities drive performance for many leaders? Why would you advocate eliminating them?"

There are two kinds of people in the world: (1) those with insecurities, and (2) those with massive insecurities. The total elimination of insecurities in any of us is impossible. They're part of the human condition. The trick is managing them in a healthy way.

Yes, some people—leaders and otherwise—are driven to great accomplishments by their insecurities. But leaders relying heavily on their own insecurities are like cars speeding down a dead-end super highway. They might be able to go fast for a while, but they eventually run out of road.

Leadership success is significantly dependent on the quality of relationships with followers. In fact, being Inwardly Sound and Others Focused is very much about creating an atmosphere in which healthy relationships can thrive. Big insecurities that have not been dealt with are a detriment to relational health. They can cause us to use others to quiet our own sense of inadequacy. Over the long haul, this leads to unhealthy relationships. And as relationships deteriorate or fail to flourish, the leader's potential is never realized.

*3/4 OF YOUR EFFECTIVENESS AS A LEADER COMES FROM WHO YOU ARE, NOT WHAT YOU DO

We all have insecurities. And, yes, at times they drive us to do great things. But, as leaders, if we lean on them too heavily for too long, we'll never find our way back to the road of unlimited potential.

MYTHS AND MISUNDERSTANDINGS #11

"Isn't Who* Not What the same thing as 'Level 5 Leadership'
and 'First Who . . . Then What?' in Jim Collins's
book Good to Great?"

Through his research and writing, many have come to know Jim Collins as one of the most influential business thinkers of the early 21st century. His books have been read by millions of people and translated into multiple languages for the entire world to consume. He has influenced countless leaders with his thinking and conclusions. Collins's influence is so pervasive that it is worth pausing to note how Who* Not What differs from "Level 5 Leadership" and "First Who . . . Then What" from Collins's book Good to Great.

It's important to note that "Level 5 Leadership" and "First Who . . . Then What" are two different ideas, so we'll address them separately. Let's begin by looking at "Level 5 Leadership."

The term "Level 5 Leadership" comes from Collins's research, which showed that the top leaders of the best organizations simultaneously hold personal humility and a steely dedication to the success of the organization that Collins calls "professional will." Collins refers to this combination as a "paradoxical blend." He says it's an important success driver for companies that achieved exceptional financial results over the long haul.[11]

While this finding was (and is) fascinating, it's not the same as the principle of *Who* Not What*. Though humility is a critical component of becoming an exceptional leader, it's not nearly enough to account for all that is needed to be Inwardly Sound and Others Focused. Even if we add to humility the courage and grit that drives the "professional will" Collins wrote about, it's not enough to account for all that is needed to be Inwardly Sound and Others Focused. In that scenario, being attentive, curious, empathic, agapone, emotionally mature, secure-and-settled, self-aware, holistically healthy, purposeful, and three of the five aspects of being principled would still be missing. As outlined in Chapters 5, 6, and 7, each of these plays an important role in becoming a well-developed *Who*.

Though we could infer that many of the characteristics of leaders who are Inwardly Sound and Others Focused were present within the most successful leaders Collins researched, inferring would be all we could do. Collins's work did not dive into the realities of who these exceptional leaders were as people beyond humility and professional will. Collins's work essentially comes to the shoreline of the truth of *Who* Not What* but stops short of getting into the water and swimming out into its depths. The truth of *Who* Not What* cannot be accurately or fully represented through Collins's concept of "Level 5 Leadership."

So, what about "First Who . . . Then What"? Doesn't that concept mimic the truth of *Who* Not What*? Though an important and valuable idea, "First Who . . . Then What" is actually further away from *Who* Not What* than "Level 5 Leadership."

"First Who . . . Then What" is a concept that Collins observed in the organizational strategies of the most successful companies he researched. Collins and his research team found that the most successful organizations were more interested in finding the best talent that was a cultural fit than finding the best talent to fill specific roles within the organization.

The belief of these high performing leaders and organizations was that the precise roles of the right players could be determined after they were hired. Not having a currently open role or knowing the precise role ahead of time wasn't a hiring deterrent for the companies with the best financial performance over the long haul. Collins and his research team concluded it was more important to "get the right people on the bus" than to pass on hiring them because it was unclear exactly what roles they would play if they were hired.

Additionally, the right people—those who were talented and a cultural fit—could even play a critical role in helping to determine the directions of their new role and company. As Collins wrote, the right people need to come ". . . before vision, before strategy, before organizational structure, before tactics."[12]

"First Who . . . Then What" is an important observation about highly successful organizations. But, despite its similar language, it is not analogous to the *Who* Not What Principle*. "First Who . . . Then What" is an organizational strategy, where *Who* Not What* is a leadership principle.

MYTHS AND MISUNDERSTANDINGS #12

"Of course I'm Inwardly Sound and Others Focused."

Mary was a leader with great potential for impact in her organization. She had a skill set and knowledge level in internet marketing that her new company needed. She was poised to positively impact the entire organization by leading them into a higher order of performance with her specialized experience.

As Mary got to know the people in her new company, comments began to swirl. Mary seemed to have little appreciation for the knowledge others had. Her style communicated to those around her that she knew best with or without their input. To be sure, Mary needed their input. Though she knew volumes about internet marketing, she knew very little about the ins and outs of her new company's core business, die cast manufacturing.

People within the organization began to have a sincere distaste for Mary. They stopped caring about her specialized knowledge because her "I know best" attitude demeaned them. Eventually, Mary's lack of interest and appreciation for her peers was too much to overcome. Instead of leading the company into a new age of marketing and business development, Mary was fired.

In the midst of this situation, I had a quiet conversation with Mary. We were discussing *Who* Not What* and how it was playing out for her. She shared with me that because she was doing her job, she was Others Focused. She reasoned that if she did her job well, the company would get better, and if the company improved, that would help everyone who worked there. Therefore, she concluded, simply by executing the tasks of her role, she was Others Focused.

Mary's beliefs about what it means to be Others Focused eliminated the very essence of what it actually is. It exchanged relational health for a business transaction. It deleted the personal care and concern that earns the energetic trust and followership of others. And it made her a very ineffective leader.

This example points directly to our final myth and

---

misunderstanding about *Who* Not What*. This myth assumes that the person we see when we look in the mirror is Inwardly Sound and Others Focused. Like the siren's song, the assumption that we are already Inwardly Sound and Others Focused seduces our egos and emotions. It invites us to write stories and develop logic that support the positive beliefs we have about ourselves as leaders, just as Mary did. If we fully buy into the assumption that we are Inwardly Sound and Others Focused, we doom our development as leaders to stagnation or worse.

Though most of us could go back through the detailed descriptions in Chapters 5, 6, and 7 and find moments in our lives when we've embodied each concept within Inwardly Sound and Others Focused, a more mature response is for us to ask ourselves, "When have I not lived this out well? When have I not been Inwardly Sound? When have I not been Others Focused?"

Time and again I've worked with leaders who, when confronted with truths in business, leadership, and life, spend their mental energy recalling the stories and examples of how they've done well rather than looking for the places where they could improve. This self-protection does little good. It buys a short-term emotional win at the expense of long-term growth and improvement.

A manuscript reviewer of this book—a leader with enormous potential—put it this way: "It is too easy to read the examples of Inwardly Sound and Others Focused and think *I have that under control*. The fact is most don't but think they do." Watch out for believing this myth. It is likely the most dangerous of them all.

With these myths and misunderstandings addressed, let's take a look at our final examples of *Who* Not What* in action. This time we'll keep a special emphasis on what it's like to be on the receiving end of leadership, both good and bad.

"Our job is only to hold up the mirror—to tell and show the public what has happened."

WALTER CRONKITE

CHAPTER TEN

Two for the Show

FINAL EXAMPLES OF BEING ON THE RECEIVING END
OF *WHO* NOT WHAT*

Early in my career, I had the good fortune of working with the executive team of Heikindo Toys in Southern California. During the engagement, I spent a fair amount of time with Heikindo's Director of Research and Development, Chen. Chen was a 13-year veteran of Heikindo and had been in his current role for five years.

One morning, I was present for a Heikindo executive meeting where Chen and a member of his R&D team, Bei, shared the details of a new, multi-year research initiative. At one point in the conversation, the president of the company asked Chen and Bei about the completion date for the research. Chen gave one answer. Bei gave a different answer. The two then acknowledged they had some differing assumptions they needed to discuss in order to determine the actual completion date. Heikindo isn't a hardcore culture that punishes people for moments like that. And in light of the overall scope of the project and what it promised to deliver, the exact completion date was a minor detail. No one in the room seemed concerned about Chen and Bei still needing to nail down this final detail.

Later that day, I sat in on a conversation between Chen and Bei. They were talking about what seemed to be run-of-the-mill items when the topic of the morning's executive meeting came up. Chen's demeanor shifted. He became visibly uneasy and chose his words carefully.

They discussed the completion date and discovered they still weren't on the same page and would have to meet again to hash out the decision. Then Chen said something to Bei that floored me:

"Bei, I need to start protecting myself now . . . oh, and you, too."

Chen talked about the mix-up that emerged during the executive meeting and how he and Bei were now under a microscope. Bei was surprised. "I don't want protection, Chen. I don't need it." But Chen insisted something dangerous had happened during that executive meeting—their reputations and credibility were on the line, and concern about fallout was a top priority.

BEGINNING OF THE END

Years later, Bei told me that when Chen said it was time to crank up the self-protection machine, it was the start of her walk out the door at Heikindo. From that day forward, Chen required updates and controls on Bei's research that were dramatically more stringent than they'd been previously. Up until then, Chen had given Bei lots of freedom because Bei was an expert in toys for children under the age of four, which was not an area in which Chen was experienced. But after that day, Chen's reporting requirements to Bei increased tenfold.

Bei's relationship with Chen began unraveling. From Bei's

perspective, Chen was inventing problems to put in Bei's performance reviews by blowing events out of proportion, ignoring simple explanations, and omitting critical details in order to tell more dramatic stories about Bei's developmental needs. Struggling with the inaccuracy of the stories Chen documented about her, Bei asked if the performance reviews could focus less on the past and more on improvement efforts for the future. Chen refused, saying, "People tend to forget what actually happened. We need to keep

"BEI, I NEED TO START PROTECTING MYSELF NOW... OH, AND YOU, TOO."
— CHEN

the stories in there." In response, Bei requested that the omitted portions of the stories be included in the documentation. Again, Chen refused.

Within 24 months, Bei, who had been told by no fewer than half of the executives at Heikindo that she was executive material—most of them saying explicitly that she had presidential capabilities—resigned from the company. She had personal reasons for leaving that had nothing to do with Chen, but told me privately, "Had I not had those reasons, I would've left anyway. I was running into Chen's issues so often that it was making my life hell. I couldn't stay there. I couldn't work for him any longer."

When I asked Bei if she had shared that with Heikindo in her exit interview, she said, "No. I was leaving for personal reasons, first and foremost. Plus, they didn't ask me any questions about Chen, so I was able to keep my integrity without talking about the mayhem of working for him. And, honestly, if I could keep my integrity without getting into all that Chen stuff, that's what I preferred. I wanted to keep a good relationship with Hei-kindo, and getting into Chen's issues wouldn't have helped in that regard. Chen has been there for a long time. It seems like no one there cares enough to see or address what's going on with him. I think it would've been foolish to put my relationship with Heikindo at risk if the executives there weren't going to take any action based on what I shared."

What had happened? What could account for Chen's behavior?

THE COST OF INSECURITY

If we're to become true students of leadership, when we encounter curious leadership behavior like Chen's, we must ask ourselves not just what happened but *why* it happened. Why did a small question from the president produce such an unusually strong response in Chen? Why was Chen's next move to create excessive controls on Bei where there once were none? And why did all this coincide with a series of truth-twisted performance reviews?

Answer: Insecurity—specifically Chen's.

Chen was scared and threatened. He had unresolved fears about interacting with his president and leading Bei. Additionally, Chen shared with me that he wasn't certain that he deserved to be in his position as an executive. Identity issues like these eat leaders—and their followers—alive if they go unresolved. When the president of the company asked a relatively benign question that didn't yet have an answer, Chen's inner-self panicked and started a chain reaction that eventually made Bei's life at the company unbearable.

Chen's comment to Bei about self-protection was telling.

Chen said it was time for him to start protecting himself, and that's exactly what he did. He did so by systematically, though probably unconsciously, destroying a relationship with an employee of high potential in order to pacify his own insecurities as a leader. And Heikindo is none the wiser about what happened.

In the two years following that executive meeting, where do you think Chen's focus was when it came to working with Bei? Was it on doing what was best for Heikindo, or was it on making sure he didn't look bad? So long as Chen's focus was on self-protection, he wasn't able to objectively assess what was in Heikindo's best interest regarding any project in which Bei was involved. In fact, Bei told me that as she and Chen worked through setting the final completion date for that research initiative, Chen never talked about which completion date would create the most value for the company. He only cared about which completion date looked good to the other executives. As Bei shared that, I saw dejection in her eyes. She said, "Weren't we supposed to make decisions based on what was best for Heikindo?"

POTENTIAL TO REPEAT ITSELF

Chen's lack of being Inwardly Sound compromised his effectiveness as a leader. His insecurities invited him to focus on himself rather than Bei or Heikindo. And, unfortunately, he accepted that invitation. Looking forward, if Chen doesn't wrestle with and resolve his insecurity demons, they will continue to haunt his direct reports and Heikindo.

Though the magnitude of Chen's reaction may sound extreme (and it was!), the core of Chen's story is not. Many leaders struggle with insecurity without any thought about how it hurts

*3/4 OF YOUR EFFECTIVENESS AS A LEADER COMES FROM WHO YOU ARE, NOT WHAT YOU DO

their followers and organizations. Insecurity hinders focus on organizational objectives and debilitates the leaders' ability to be Others Focused for his or her followers. To make matters even worse, insecurity is difficult to see in the mirror. We lie to ourselves about our insecurities. We give them other names and rationalize them away. But they are, at their core, personal qualities that deeply damage our effectiveness as leaders.

MANY LEADERS STRUGGLE WITH INSECURITY WITHOUT ANY THOUGHT ABOUT HOW IT HURTS THEIR FOLLOWERS AND ORGANIZATIONS.

Before we leave Chen, it's worth acknowledging one final reality: He didn't wake up every morning wanting to feel insecure. His unique combination of talents, personality, and, most importantly, life experiences, led him there. Imagine what it would be like to show up at work each and every day feeling scared, threatened, and inadequate. If you've ever experienced that, you know the anxiety and stress it causes. Bei was angry with Chen, but sympathy—or better yet, empathy—would have been a more helpful response.

If we don't or can't mature out of our insecurities, we would do ourselves and our organizations a favor by finding different leadership roles to play—roles that don't inflame those insecurities. Doing so would be an example of an admirable component of being Inwardly Sound—self-aware.

Bei's story of being on the receiving end of Chen's insecure leadership is a vivid example of *Who* * *Not What* in action. Let's take a look at another example with a happier ending.

PEDRO'S STORY

On a Monday morning a few years ago, a close friend of mine named Pedro sent me this text:

> *"I am done with this. I just had our VP come in and ask me how my weekend was. I said, 'My 8 hours of cost accounting on Saturday was surprisingly painless,' to which he responded, 'I need you doing [expletive] sales not [expletive] cost accounting.' What is sad is that in the office/business I am known for having the best relationship with him. I am the ombudsman for anything that needs to be transmitted to or from our VP."*

Let me share a little bit about Pedro. He's the 32-year-old North and South American Sales Director for a fertilizer distribution company. When he sent that text, he was working in his spare time on an Executive MBA at one of the world's most prestigious schools (thus the reference to cost accounting in his text). Pedro is incredibly book smart, but also so grounded with common sense that it's almost annoying. From an entry-level sales position, he quickly rose through the ranks of his organization. He was not only the sales leader for two continents, but also a trusted resource for those in the transportation and accounting departments. This is in large part because of his uncanny ability to connect with people better than just about anyone I've ever encountered.

Some time ago, I was on an overseas trip with Pedro. We were part of a small group of people visiting a rural community for a week. While there, we interacted with local children through skits and sports. At one point, our entire group realized Pedro was nowhere to be found. We didn't panic, but there was concern. Then, out of the corner of my eye, I saw what looked like a horse galloping among the dappled rays of sunlight in the forest. Pedro was on that horse. A few minutes later, he came walking back to our group. We asked what had happened. Pedro matter-of-factly explained that a local farmer had lost his horse. Pedro had helped him find it. He couldn't even speak the farmer's language, but that didn't stop him from making a connection. Pedro's ability to sincerely connect with almost anyone is rare. His capacity to be both relational and strategic invites most business people who meet him to immediately want Pedro on their team.

AVOIDING CONFRONTATION

Now recall the first sentence of Pedro's text: "I am done with this." How does someone with such talent end up so frustrated? Wouldn't those around him ensure he had all the space and support he needed to flourish? Wouldn't they remember what they saw in him when they hired him and what they had experienced since his arrival? Apparently not.

To understand what moved Pedro to send that text, let's travel back in time to a couple of weeks before he sent it. Pedro was invited, as he often was, to a meeting above his pay grade and formal title. He sat with the company president, Luciana, and vice presidents discussing the organization's inability to keep its bagging and packaging equipment running reliably. They were losing sales and clients. It was not a happy day.

During the discussion, Pedro confronted Luciana, who, months earlier, had promised to free up some much-needed physical space in the manufacturing area. It was a simple commitment that only required communication with the maintenance department. Luciana attempted to use her power as the company's president to sidestep Pedro's questioning, but Pedro wouldn't have it. He kept pressing Luciana for a commitment to free up the needed space. Luciana finally confessed that she was the bottleneck and ended the meeting without a resolution.

Figure 18: Reporting Relationships Between Pedro, Alejandro, and Luciana

Luciana left the building and didn't return to work the following day. She was unable or unwilling to deal with this basic confrontation. Despite her position as president, Luciana was underdeveloped as a person.

Alejandro, the vice president mentioned in Pedro's frustrated text message, had been less than impressive for Pedro's entire time at the company. His business trips around the globe defined his sense of self-worth. He was a middle-aged man with sad aspirations of being an international playboy. He was careless with company funds and indulgent when it came to personal expenses. His vice presidential perspective on the business was limited to "Sell! Sell! Sell!" He was not exactly an intellectual giant or strategic savant. Beyond introductions to clients and telling Pedro how to cheat on expense reports, Alejandro offered nothing in terms of coaching, growth, or development to Pedro.

OUT OF CONTROL AND UNCHECKED

It would be easy to point the finger at Alejandro as the source of Pedro's dissatisfaction. But Alejandro wasn't actually first in line. Luciana was. Luciana's inability to handle confrontation was the key issue. This shortcoming—not in business strategy but in human development—was the major impediment to keeping talented individuals such as Pedro in the organization. This underdeveloped aspect of Luciana has been a problem for years. It's what allowed Alejandro to operate as he did—out of control and unchecked. Pedro's text, which marked the beginning of his exit from the company, was fueled by a lack of personal development in Luciana.

This is a perfect example of how who we are as people is responsible for 3/4 of our success and failure as leaders. Who we are *really* matters in leadership. Its effects aren't relegated to theory or philosophy. They're real. Just read Pedro's text again to see it in action.

FULL CONFIDENCE

About six months after he sent that text to me, Pedro completed his Executive MBA studies. Being the sharp, emerging leader he was, he had numerous employment opportunities. Not one ounce of him wanted to stay under Alejandro's and

Luciana's leadership.

Leveraging his newly acquired education with his international sales experience, Pedro accepted the position of Global Business Development Director for an international soybean producer. I had the opportunity to visit with him after he'd been in his new position for a year. I asked him about the difference between the leaders and cultures of his old and new companies. Here are a few of his thoughts:

> *"It's night-and-day different. I used to be embarrassed by the things that went on at my office. Now, I'm proud of what I'm trying to work through, the stuff I'm getting to do, and the people I work with. At my old company, I wouldn't have wanted to introduce the owner or my co-workers to anyone."*

> *"The character of my current boss? He's a stud. He doesn't put up with anything. It's known that if you make a nasty quip in an email about someone, he'll send it to that person and ask about the comment you made . . . as if to say, 'I think we should discuss this. There might be an issue here.' He has zero tolerance for gossip or unhealthy communication. So it just doesn't exist. At my old organization, the president was talking s--- about everyone behind their backs."*

> *"[My current boss] drives me harder than I've ever been driven, but it's good. I like it. I trust him. I have full confidence in his character and his competence."*

"I'm given opportunities that challenge me and stretch me as opposed to being thrust into messed-up situations all the time."

"[My current boss] expects you to act as a person of character and treat others well. He doesn't tolerate people treating one another in a crappy fashion—nor do any of the executives. [At the old company], we had just bickering and stupid . . . just high schoolish [stuff]. [At my new company], we don't have all that unhealthiness going on because the owner doesn't tolerate it. There's a trickle-down effect."

"The business impact of not tolerating unhealthy communication and poisonous relationships is that we're more efficient. Immature and selfish communication is inefficient and ineffective. There was a bunch of that crap going on at [my old company]. You had to couch everything [you said] and [worry], 'Is somebody in a bad mood?' At [my new company], that kind of stuff is just not tolerated."

Those are impressive comments about Pedro's new leaders and company. He saw and felt the difference healthy leaders make. He made the connection not only to his own role as a follower, but also to all aspects of his new company. This is worth exploring for a few moments.

HEALTH CREATES EFFICIENCY

Business author and consultant Patrick Lencioni opens his book,

The Advantage: Why Organizational Health Trumps Everything Else in Business, by saying, "The single greatest advantage any company can achieve is organizational health." He goes on to write, "The health of an organization provides the context for strategy, finance, marketing, technology, and everything else that happens within it, which is why it is the single greatest factor determining an organization's success. More than talent. More than knowledge. More than innovation."[1]

> **"THE BUSINESS IMPACT OF NOT TOLERATING UNHEALTHY COMMUNICATION AND POISONOUS RELATIONSHIPS IS THAT WE'RE MORE EFFICIENT."**
> **— PEDRO**

Lencioni is describing the organizational version of *Who* * *Not What*. He's determined that health within organizations enables everything else that organizations do. This is an exact parallel to how being a healthy and well-developed leader enables everything else the leader does. It's what Pedro experienced in both his new and old companies—positively in his new company and negatively in his old company.

In another part of our conversation, Pedro described his new company as one of high performance based on interdependence. Then he shared this:

> "When you have that unhealthy behavior going on like at my old company, interdependence isn't safe. If I can't trust you, I can't depend on you. So I'll mitigate you, go around you, because there's no way I can work with you.
>
> "Here [in my new company], there's an extraordinary

---

*3/4 OF YOUR EFFECTIVENESS AS A LEADER COMES FROM WHO YOU ARE, NOT WHAT YOU DO

*amount of trust that everyone will do his or her part,
follow through, do what's right for the organization and
not just for the individual. It creates a lot of efficiencies.
When you tolerate unhealthy behavior, it destroys trust.
And where trust is absent, everything becomes more
inefficient."*

There it is again, that word: *efficiency.* It appears that the
words "health" and "efficiency" are joined at the hip. And now
we'll join them to "strategic advantage."

As suggested by Lencioni and confirmed by Pedro's experiences, unhealthy organizations are at a strategic disadvantage in the marketplace because they don't enjoy the same efficiencies in communication and relationships as their healthy counterparts. The highest levels of performance and efficiency between leaders and their followers require trust. High levels of trust aren't possible without well-developed leaders who create healthy relationships and healthy communication. Therefore, the highest levels of potential-fulfilling organizational performance cannot be achieved without well-developed, healthy leaders.

Leaders who are inwardly unsound and self-focused don't have the ability to create healthy, trusting organizations. Organizations can't reach their full potential if underdeveloped or unhealthy leaders are leading them. To think they could is to suggest that the most basic principles of human interaction and influence have magically become untrue.

The health of our organizations and their subsequent efficiencies have everything to do with how healthy and well developed our leaders are. We can accurately say that the truth of *Who* Not What* not only parallels Lencioni's observations, but it enables them as well. Healthy, well-developed organizations are created by healthy, well-developed leaders. Look at Pedro's comments about his new company. What do you see? Well-developed leaders whose personal qualities created a healthy and efficient organization.

MORE NUMBERS

At the end of the conversation, I asked Pedro to compare his first year under his current leaders at his new company to his final year under his previous leaders at his old company. I asked him to rate three factors on a scale of 1 to 10, with 10 being the highest rating (Table 3).

	PREVIOUS LEADERS	CURRENT LEADERS
Enjoyment of the job	2	7.5
Personal learning and development	2	10
Long-term prospects with the company	1	9

Table 3: Pedro's Old and New Company Comparison

The effects of well-developed leaders on both followers and organizational efficiency can't be overstated. Pedro, a supremely talented and high-potential leader, is now on the receiving end of well-developed leaders, and he's loving it. As always, whether in good or bad leaders, *Who* Not What* is doing its thing.

*3/4 OF YOUR EFFECTIVENESS AS A LEADER COMES FROM WHO YOU ARE, NOT WHAT YOU DO

"Always do your best. What you plant now, you will harvest later."

OG MANDINO

CHAPTER ELEVEN

So What? Now What?

LEVERAGING THE TRUTH OF *WHO* NOT WHAT*

What are we to do with all of these concepts, data, and examples? How can we leverage the truth of *Who* Not What?* Let's start with us as followers.

1. Leverage the truth of *Who* Not What* to help us choose who we will follow.

When considering who we'll follow in the workplace or other realms of life, we'd do well to remember how much our leaders affect the quality of our lives. Their impact is profound. But following leaders who are Inwardly Sound and Others Focused is not merely a more enjoyable experience. These leaders also produce better results. Over the long haul, all other things being equal, they get more done.

There is no doubt it's difficult—if not impossible—to get a read on the inner development of your potential new boss in a 45-minute interview. But a little *Who* Not What* recon can be done, especially by those considering new positions within their current firms. If at all possible, ask those who have worked for your potential new boss what it's like to follow that person.

A non-threatening way to learn about the foibles you might encounter is to ask, "When [your potential new leader] is not at their best, what does it look like and what does the team do to help and support [your potential new leader] in those moments?" Another method is to ask about the most rewarding aspects of following that leader. In all cases, listen intently for answers that suggest how much of a well-developed *Who* your potential new leader is. And if you're feeling really bold, you could even show a current follower of that leader a list of the 11 qualities that make up an Inwardly Sound and Others Focused leader and ask how much the leader in question embodies those qualities.

Wisely choosing who we follow is critical. Remember that even as they are interviewing you for a new role, you are interviewing someone to be your new leader. As you do, be on the lookout for indicators of the deeper realties of being Inwardly Sound and Others Focused. It's a must now that we've identified the ever-present reality of *Who* * Not *What*.

2. Leverage the truth of *Who* * Not *What* to help us develop other leaders.

It's my hope that putting a name to the reality of *Who* * Not *What* fundamentally impacts the discussions you have with those you are responsible for developing as leaders. If we're to help our followers reach their potential as leaders, we cannot be content with conversations that go no deeper than the *What* of leadership. If we're to develop world-class leaders, we must have world-class conversations about leadership. If those conversations are to be effective and truly developmental, they must dive deeply into the issues of motive, ego, humility, self-interest, self-preservation, and all other aspects of being Inwardly Sound and Others Focused.

If *Who* the leader is comprises 3/4 of leadership, we could argue that 3/4 of leader development efforts should be directed at helping up-and-coming leaders become more Inwardly Sound and Others Focused. Many may be fearful of such meaty and challenging conversations. But I fear *that fear* is what has kept *Who* Not What* hidden for so long. The future will belong to the leaders and organizations that have the courage to bring

IF WE'RE TO DEVELOP WORLD-CLASS LEADERS, WE MUST HAVE WORLD-CLASS CONVERSATIONS ABOUT LEADERSHIP.

the truth of *Who* Not What* into the light as they develop their leaders.

You may be responsible for leader development, not just at a one-on-one level, but also at an enterprise level. You may be a chief executive officer, president, senior vice president, executive, chief learning officer, human resources leader, division head, department head, or team lead. If so, I want to repeat a statement you just read, but with special emphasis this time: The future will belong to the leaders *and organizations* that have the courage to bring the truth of *Who* Not What* into the light as they develop their leaders.

Those who are responsible for influencing and choosing the substance of leader development within their organizations have the opportunity to systematically integrate the truth of *Who* Not What* into their organizations. Regardless of the type of development—formal or informal, daily or multi-annually, experiential or classroom—leaders who are serious about helping

*3/4 OF YOUR EFFECTIVENESS AS A LEADER COMES FROM WHO YOU ARE, NOT WHAT YOU DO

their organizations reach their full potential must create leader development content and methods that embrace and address the reality of *Who* Not What*.

Those of us who are sincerely dedicated to developing great leaders must regularly and intentionally engage in conversations with our followers about becoming more Inwardly Sound and Others Focused. Their leadership potential can't be fully realized without it.

3. Leverage the truth of *Who* Not What* to help us develop ourselves as leaders.

The truth of *Who* Not What* is a mirror. It can help you see yourself accurately . . . if you're willing to look. Many leaders aren't, because taking a cold, hard look at ourselves is difficult. But it's the only way to order our own development if we want to reach our full potential as leaders.

When you look at each of essential aspects of leadership listed in The Leadership Tree (Figure 6 on page 57), would you estimate that 3/4 of your current efforts to develop yourself as a leader are in the areas of Inwardly Sound and Others Focused? If the answer is no, don't sweat it. Almost no one is approaching their own development that way. But armed with this information, you now have the opportunity to separate yourself from your peers by aiming your personal leadership development efforts at their most valuable targets. It will take courage to do so, but courage is actually a character quality of Inwardly Sound leaders. Look at that—the very act of starting down this path has given you the opportunity to grow in courage. Congratulations! You're already making progress.

Of course, this path of leader development is more difficult than simply getting started. It takes time. "How much time?" you ask. I'll answer that with a question: How long does it take a strong, prosperous tree to grow?

Developing yourself as a person is a lifetime endeavor. It requires depth, community and time. We need depth because we can't adequately develop our *Who* without investigating our motives and perspectives. We need community to (1) hold us accountable to the consistent and difficult effort required to grow as a person, (2) offer us wise perspectives and observations that may differ from our own, and (3) help us learn from others' *Who* journeys. And we need time because the vast majority of personal growth takes time: time to understand thoroughly, time to try, time to fail, time to try again, time to succeed, and time to repeat that success.

LEADERS WHO ARE SERIOUS ABOUT HELPING THEIR ORGANIZATIONS REACH THEIR FULL POTENTIAL MUST CREATE LEADER DEVELOPMENT CONTENT AND METHODS THAT EMBRACE AND ADDRESS THE REALITY OF *WHO* NOT WHAT*.

This last point—the need for time—may be especially disappointing to many given we live in a world where Google gives us search results before we've even finished typing a query, and delayed gratification is seen as a quaint ideal from days of yore. But our disappointment doesn't change the facts: it takes time and effort to become a well-developed person who leads well. We

*3/4 OF YOUR EFFECTIVENESS AS A LEADER COMES FROM WHO YOU ARE, NOT WHAT YOU DO

must be committed and patient if we're to reach our full leadership potential.

4. Understanding *Who* Not What* helps us become the best leaders we can be. Those following us desperately need that.

I actually expect I won't be able to write this last section without it bringing me to tears. Almost every time I start to cover what I'm about to share with you—even if I'm practicing for a talk alone in my car—I get emotional. That's how deeply I feel about the paragraphs that follow.

Recently, I discovered my passion for leaders isn't my deepest motivation in the work I do. My deepest motivation is followers. We've all been followers. We've all been profoundly affected by the leaders we've followed. My colleague, John Ott, who I referenced earlier in the book, says that leadership is "the stewardship of power and opportunity." I believe that's an exceptionally accurate definition for something everyone and his brother seems to want to redefine.

I especially like John's definition for how it acknowledges the power that leaders hold. There's little, if anything, on this earth that affects our day-to-day experiences more than the leaders we follow. They have the power to make our days hard or easy, fulfilling or pointless, fun or painful. And they do so every day. Our leaders do this for (or to) us and we do it for (or to) the people we lead.

To have such a profound and tangible effect on another person's life on a daily basis makes leadership a privileged responsibility. As John's definition suggests, it's something we get to steward. It's a privilege to do so. Not everyone gets to enjoy that privilege.

GOING HOME

Let's think about the people who follow us for just a moment. Tonight, when they go home from work, what are they going home to? Some may go home to bliss and ease, but most go home to life—real life. And real life can be tough. Some are taking care of ill parents. Others are caring for ill children. Still others are facing health challenges of their own. Some of those health challenges are short-term annoyances, while others are more serious.

Many of the people we lead go home to breaking or broken relationships. Connections with teenage children are fractured and need to be repaired. Others are only beginning their parenting journey and are in a constant state of elevated nerves and sleep deprivation. Some would give everything they have just to be able to have a child to keep them up at night.

TO HAVE SUCH A PROFOUND AND TANGIBLE EFFECT ON ANOTHER PERSON'S LIFE ON A DAILY BASIS MAKES LEADERSHIP A PRIVILEGED RESPONSIBILITY.

Many of our followers go home to frayed marriages. Some are only frayed for the moment, but others have been frayed for a long time. Maybe someone has been cheated on. Perhaps someone has done the cheating. Someone may have moved out of the house to live elsewhere. For some, the divorce papers are about to be served. Others are giving it one last try.

And then there are the typical challenges that come with

*3/4 OF YOUR EFFECTIVENESS AS A LEADER COMES FROM WHO YOU ARE, NOT WHAT YOU DO

family. Relationships with in-laws and siblings rarely come without at least some complication. Family-of-origin dynamics play out in so many—and often difficult—ways. Some of those who follow us feel the challenge of living long distances from their families-of-origin, while others might be healthier if they lived farther away from their relatives.

The loneliness of singleness is heavy for some of our followers. Others are dying to get out of unhealthy dating relationships, but they don't know how. Some are watching loved ones struggle with substance abuse, while others are struggling with substance abuse themselves. Still others are fighting off memories of sexual or emotional abuse. For some, those memories are not so distant.

And let's not forget about money. Some of our followers wrestle with the burden of student loans or consumer debt. Some are trying to repair credit scores while funding their children's education. Others are trying to absorb large and unexpected medical bills or home repairs. Whether brought on by unwise choices or forces outside their control, financial insecurity is a stressful bedmate for many of our followers.

Life is full of challenges—not in theory, but in reality. Want to know how I know that? It's because these are the same challenges we all face. Whether leader or follower, as members of the human race, we all experience setbacks and hurdles like the ones listed above. And if you sit in the seat of leadership at any level in any organization, you know that doing so hasn't exempted you from life's difficulties.

As we look back on the leaders in our lives, here are some questions to consider:

- Have the leaders we've followed enabled us to better handle the challenges of life, or have they made them more difficult?
- Did they send us home at the end of the day more fully ourselves or less?
- Did they send us to our doorsteps in the evening depleted in every way, or ready to be the best wives, husbands, mothers, fathers, daughters, sons, or friends we're capable of being?
- Have the leaders we've followed dominated our dinner table conversations because of the positives they've brought into our lives or because of the pain they've created?
- Can we look back and say we were thankful to have followed those leaders as the challenges of life came at us, or would we say those leaders themselves were the challenges we faced?

I, for one, have had both experiences. I've had leaders who filled me up. I've had leaders who drained me. I've had leaders who made me a better person by intention. I've had leaders whose only purpose for me was to make their lives more comfortable and productive.

I enjoy great organizational culture. I value revenues and profits. I esteem efficiency. And I love that exceptional leadership can produce all of these. But I've discovered that my deepest passion within leadership is for *followers* and what they have left to invest in their worlds after having been led by us. Perhaps that's exactly as it should be. After all, leadership wouldn't exist without followers.

*3/4 OF YOUR EFFECTIVENESS AS A LEADER COMES FROM WHO YOU ARE, NOT WHAT YOU DO

AN AMAZING OPPORTUNITY

The power we carry as leaders is significant. It has a daily effect that will leave lifelong marks on those we lead. Though I've failed in meaningful ways in the past, I can say it's my heart's desire to not only achieve great organizational results through leadership, but also to make the lives of those I'm leading more livable, more energetic, and better prepared to deal with life's challenges.

If you're wondering why you should embark on the challenging journey of becoming a well-developed leader—an exceptional *Who*—I invite you to look at the faces of those you lead and perhaps even imagine the faces of those you will lead in the future. They, and the friends and family members they influence every day, are worth our best efforts to become the best leaders we can be. No matter how much some of them may sometimes frustrate us, they're worth it. They're going through the same life challenges we've experienced. In that sense, they aren't followers; they're our peers, fellow travelers in life.

Leveraging the truth about leadership—that 3/4 of our effectiveness as leaders comes from *Who* we are, not *What* we do—in order to become extraordinary leaders isn't about the story our followers will tell about us. It's about how much better their lives will be if we lead them well—if we lead them as leaders who are Inwardly Sound and Others Focused. If we can be exceptional leaders for them, they will feel the effects of it long after they've left our charge. Exceptional leadership echoes throughout the lives of our followers. Poor leadership does so as well. Let's use the power we've been given as leaders to echo well.

"Take the first step in faith. You don't have to see the whole staircase, just take the first step."

MARTIN LUTHER KING, JR.

EPILOGUE

First, thank you for reading *The Only Leaders Worth* Following*. It is a deep passion of mine to share these thoughts with the world. By reading this book, you've given me the opportunity to do just that.

Second, as I mentioned in the Introduction, this is not a how-to book. That doesn't mean it's a book of theories floated to see if anyone agrees with them. Its ideas are, as you have seen, far more verifiable than that. But a how-to book it is not. It does not include volumes of exercises on how to become more Inwardly Sound and Others Focused. This was done purposefully.

Though I have had the privilege of working with leaders on multiple continents in practices and methods for becoming more well-developed *Whos*, I didn't want the book to be a checklist of developmental methodologies. I wanted to keep the book focused squarely on the truth and depth of the *Who* Not What Principle* so that you, its readers, could marinate in its ideas. In my view, this drives the understanding of its principles deeper than they would go if we were creating a list of to-dos throughout the book. Thus, the book is intended to first display the reality of the *Who* Not What Principle* and then invite you to begin ongoing conversations with yourself and others about it.

The "how-to" of becoming as Inwardly Sound and Others Focused as we can be is challenging, but not impossible. For all of human history, people have grown and developed over the course of their lives—not just in experience but within the depths of who they are. As time passes, our perspectives, beliefs, and souls can change. Ask almost any person you know if they think, believe, and see the world today exactly as they did five years ago. Very few will say they do. The question then isn't *if* we can become more well-developed people in order to become better leaders, but *how*.

Perhaps the most common question this book's readers ask is, "I see it. I get it. I agree. But what do I do?" The answer depends on the unique circumstances of each person or organization asking the question. Different personal experiences and organizational cultures carry with them different baggage and challenges. Additionally, whether as individuals, departments, or companies, we have different levels of potential based on a variety of factors. The best leadership development—especially at the *Who* level—is deeply personalized.

That said, there are some general practices that serve well the individuals and organizations that desire to reach their leadership potential. One simple strategy is to become a master of asking, "Why?" When we see effective or ineffective leadership—whether individually and organizationally—we can learn a great deal by asking ourselves, "Why?" over and over again until we get to the juicy center of the leaders involved.

Another strategy is to seek out those who are what we aspire to become. Of the leaders you know, who are the most Inwardly Sound and Others Focused? Take them to lunch and shower them with questions about their beliefs, perspectives, and how they became who they are.

What organizations have the healthiest, most efficient internal relationships and cultures? Ask for a conversation with those who have developed and led those cultures. Whether you're focused on individuals or organizations, tell those you're meeting with why you want to talk with them. Explain that you aspire to maximize your leadership potential. You may have to wait months for the appointment, but it is rare, in my experience, that you'll be flatly turned down. At the end of those discussions, ask them who else they think you should connect with. An exercise like this is exactly how I began my study of leadership. This approach works for heads of departments and presidents of organizations just as well as it does for 20-somethings beginning their careers. We never outgrow the need and opportunity to learn.

Lastly, I would be remiss if I didn't mention the organization I lead, The Aperio, as a resource for helping you, your team, or your organization become more Inwardly Sound and Others Focused. At the time of publication, The Aperio has cumulatively facilitated over 2,200 months of *Who*-based leadership development. This has happened with more than 250 leaders in North America, Asia, and Australia whose roles range from the most senior executive leaders to middle managers to frontline leaders. These experiences have created for us a depth of knowledge and experience about the process of becoming a more well-developed *Who* for which we are both proud and thankful. We relish sharing this knowledge and experience with others. We have seen the truth of *Who* Not What* impact the bottom lines and key metrics of our clients. We have also been humbled and fulfilled to see positive outcomes in marriages, relationships with children, and friendships through our work.

If you find yourself desiring support in the journey toward becoming a more well-developed *Who*—or improving in any aspect of The Leadership Tree—I personally invite you

*3/4 OF YOUR EFFECTIVENESS AS A LEADER COMES FROM WHO YOU ARE, NOT WHAT YOU DO

to read more about us (TheAperio.com) and reach out to contact us (Hello@TheAperio.com). The Aperio exists to help individuals and organizations within our scope of influence understand and experience truly exceptional leadership and all of the benefits that come with it, from better bottom-line results to more fulfilling lives. We would love to assist you toward that end.

I sincerely and deeply hope this book serves as a springboard to help you be and become a more well-developed *Who*, not just for your sake or the sake of your organization, but also for the sake of those who follow you. If we can achieve this, it would be no small accomplishment.

With Anticipation and Hope—

Tim Spiker

*"Feeling gratitude and not expressing
it is like wrapping a present and not giving it."*

WILLIAM ARTHUR WARD

ACKNOWLEDGMENTS

This is, by far, the scariest part of this book to write. So many people have contributed to and enabled my learning and passion for leadership. My fear is that I will forget one or more of them. Of course, there's the other side of that coin. It includes me thanking every teacher I've ever had—substitutes included—from elementary to graduate school. I'll spare us all that exercise and simply hope I don't make any relationship-ending omissions.

I'll start with the practical. To the more than 30 people who read the manuscript of this book and offered your transparent and detailed feedback, thank you. You made this book significantly better than it would have been without your input.

Thanks also to the book's editors, **Dan Mancini** and **Dana Wilkerson**. Dan, you possess a wonderful mix of challenge and flexibility. Thank you for not only your expertise, but also for your interest in the book's message and potential. Dana, your eye for detail and commitment to thoroughness made this book far better before it went out the door.

In addition to the content and copy editing of Dan and Dana, there was a group of people with editing experience who read each and every word of this book on the hunt for errors in grammar, wording, and layout. It is scary to me to think about what would have gone to print without your diligent error checking. For your efforts, a special thanks goes to the book's error editing team of **Sara Turner, Sarah Spiker, Karyl Wackerlin,**

Sabra Spiker, and Paula Moore.

I must also thank **Rob Eagar** (startawildfire.com) for his contribution to this effort. You dug into the heart of my motives for writing this book. In doing so, you unearthed a better title for the book than the one I'd been holding on to for a decade.

My next thanks goes to **Jodi Gutzmirtl**. What started with me needing administrative support "Stat!" a few years ago has turned into a valuable relationship to me, not only in terms of business, but also in life. You have encouraged me more than you know with your belief in *Who* * *Not What*. Without your support of *Who* * *Not What* journeys and The Aperio's business overall, this book would not be what it is today.

The number-one question asked of me over the last three years has been, "When is the book coming out?" Thanks to you, **Mike Davis**, there is finally an answer to that question. You are the straw that has broken the camel's back on this project—the camel being the multiple barriers in the way of getting it done. This is just the first of many projects we are going to get done together. Thanks for bringing yourself and your very unique gifting to The Aperio. (And thanks for letting him, Elloa.)

A huge thanks go to my parents, **John and Sabra Spiker**. Dad, you have been a picture of leadership worth following my entire life. You taught me more poignantly than you know that all people are to be valued. It is powerful to see that in a leader. Mom, from your example I've learned to be resourceful and committed in the endeavors to which I am called. The passion that covers my work was learned from you. To you both: Not only did you champion education and sacrifice unending hours and dollars for my academic and athletic pursuits but, even more importantly, you believed in and encouraged me without end.

No matter how crazy my ideas or dreams, you never said, "No," or, "You can't do that." The import and impact of such love and support is incalculable. Without it, this book would not exist. I am and will be forever grateful for the blessing of getting to be your son.

To my sister, **Heather Throckmorton**, thank you for your belief in me and for sharing that belief *with* me. It is inspiring. For **Zach Spiker**, my brother, thank you for teaching me how to lead a cultural change. I'm watching and learning from you.

Thank you to my in-laws, **Gary and Karyl Wackerlin**, for your encouragement about this project and its potential impact. Thank you to my siblings-in-law, **Kris Wackerlin, Emily Wackerlin, John Throckmorton,** and **Jenn Spiker**. Though you may not have previously known it or even done it on purpose, each of you, in small moments and your own unique ways, have been an encouragement to me in the pursuit of writing this book.

Along the way, there have been educators who stepped in with care and interest that exceeded what was required of them. Thank you to **Jim Field**, who made me feel like a valuable person whose ideas were worth discussing. Thank you to **Mary Fallon** and the late **Peter Friend**, who creatively invited me, a math and science kid, to see the English language as worthy of my time and attention. I owe a meaningful debt of gratitude to college professors **Andrea Heugatter** and **Stacy Jackson**. You both encouraged me to be who I was made to be. You helped give life to the talents and interests God planted in me. And though not a formal educator in my life, the investment in me by **Dave Lovell** was the first of that type I ever received. You, Dave, were the first person to suggest that I should be investing in others. Thank you for seeing something in me (and sharing it!) that I didn't see in

*3/4 OF YOUR EFFECTIVENESS AS A LEADER COMES FROM WHO YOU ARE, NOT WHAT YOU DO

myself.

A big thanks also goes to **Gene Keady**, whose leadership I described in Chapter 6. Coach, you gave me the opportunity to be a part of something very special at Purdue when most others in your position would not have given someone of my size and athleticism a chance. I am also thankful to Coach **Mark Edwards** and Assistant Coach **Kevin O'Connell** for whom I played my final two collegiate basketball seasons at Washington University in St. Louis. I am just as proud to have been a part of the basketball program at WashU as I am at having played at Purdue. I am thankful in deep ways for all of my collegiate athletic experiences and the coaches and assistant coaches who led me in them.

I have experienced few privileges in life greater than leading a group of men affectionately called the "Losers." You gave me the deep satisfaction of leading you. You not only survived me learning how to lead, but you made it fun to do so. Leading you for that season is one of the biggest honors of my life. Thank you for allowing me that opportunity. There were a variety of people involved in the early years, each unique and valuable in his own way. A group of you has chosen to stay connected for decades, and for that I want to mention you by name: **Jeff Adams, Joel Anderson, Tim Banze, Chris Birkner, Jeff Burzynski, Josh Busch, Bryan Cantu, Joel Cryder, Ryan "Nation" Henry, Bart King, John McLaughlin, Noah Oldham, Marc Sikma, Jeff Strobach,** and **Brian Warner**. I think about what each of you are doing now and am humbled to be associated with you. See you at the next BTT.

I could not complete a list of thank yous without including **Brad Simms**. Brad, though your aims with me haven't been directly in the realm of leadership, your investment in me has continually shown me the power of acceptance and care. You are a great encourager who has earned the right to challenge me to higher standards in my life. You have modeled for me how to do so with others. Your friendship has helped to make me a better person and a better leader. Also in the tribe of world-class encouragers is you, **David Wenzel**. You have an ultra-attractive ability to connect your mind to your heart. Despite your talents and unique experiences, you constantly focus on the interests and stories of others. I experience joy every time I speak with you. Thank you for blessing my life with your friendship, encouragement, and presence.

Professionally, the list of people to thank is long. Thank you to **John Brooks** for birthing a confidence in me that I didn't know existed. Thank you to **Mark Benson,** who not only taught me what it meant to be a "nutritious" person, but exemplified it as well.

Thank you to **Ron Magnus** and **Dan Wooldridge** for being the first people to give me the opportunity to professionally pursue my passion for leader development. The list of consulting colleagues and subcontractors at FMI for whom I am thankful is long enough that I won't list them all here. Thank you to all of you who endured and encouraged my early start as a consultant.

Speaking of early starts in consulting, I must recognize a group of leaders and companies called the **Peer Group**. You allowed a young, green consultant to cut his teeth in your midst. You gave me the space, despite my age and experience, to challenge you regarding leadership. Your openness to me over the years buoyed my confidence and gave me a breadth of education in real-world business that few people experience. I can only hope that you received back from me as much as I received from you.

Thanks go to you, **Bob Dude,** for taking me under your

wing. You are unparalleled in your groundedness, transparency, and soul-filled approach to your work. Thanks also to **David Mariner**. Since working for you 12 years ago, you have shown me by example the self-evaluation, consistency, and commitment to personal development indicative of an outstanding leader. Thank you, **Leigh Armstrong**, for countless hours of constructive arguments, dreams, and encouragement. In addition to being a practitioner unafraid of entering into discussions of *Who* Not What* and worldview with those you lead, you toiled with me in figuring out how to get the message of *Who* Not What* off the ground. Thank you also goes to **Dr. Tim Elmore** (growingleaders.com), whose conversations with me over the years repeatedly left me believing that what was planted within me was, in fact, valuable enough to share with the world.

In recent years, my life has been enriched in this work and in general by a group of leaders, coaches, and consultants who have joined me in striving to provide deep and rich leadership development experiences for others. Thank you to **Dr. Mary Shippy** (alignleadership.com), who has been both an informal and formal personal development coach to me. You are always generous with your time and your wise counsel impacts my life on a weekly basis. Thank you to **Chip Toth** (leadersinspire.net) for surviving my tenacity, only to love and care about me anyway. Few people can compete with your ability to listen to and coach leaders. Additional thank yous go to **Evan McLaughlin, Zach Fay, Stuart Brown,** and **Ken Brown**. You have all encouraged me in ways that I needed. Thank you, **Michelle Pape** (next-monday.com), for your encouragement and humility. I am so thankful for the unexpected cold call that brought us together. **Sam Reid** (ideas2impact.com), I both love and hate that I can never exit a meeting with you without some type of commitment to an action plan. Thank you for being an example of a wonderful and rare combination of curiosity, transparency, and intellect. You are the consummate consultant and a great example from whom I will continue to learn.

I will forever be grateful to a group of leaders at a company that wishes to remain anonymous. You offered me a wonderful opportunity. You asked me to help shape the leaders of our organization and you gave me tremendous freedom to do so. What I learned in my time with you was beyond what I thought I could learn. It extended well outside the bounds of leadership into culture and organizational dynamics. My thanks is not limited to the leaders of that company. Many, many people within the organization redefined my understanding of collaborative relationships and what it looks like to be fully committed to solutions. I will carry those understandings with me for the rest of my life. Thank you for being such great examples and teachers to me.

To the **leaders across the world at Boral,** I must thank you above any other group of leaders. You have created space for *Who* * *Not What* not only in your work but also in your lives. You have fostered opportunity after opportunity for me to learn from you even while it was my responsibility to facilitate your expeditions into *Who* * *Not What*. Your openness to share your experiences along the way has had an incalculable influence on me and this message. You and the people you lead are why this work is so fulfilling.

To the dynamic duo of **John Ott** and **Vanessa Kiley** (exceptionalleaders.com), "thank you" hardly seems to capture it. I am so appreciative of your friendship and the joy you have brought to me as we have labored together. How many hours

---

*3/4 OF YOUR EFFECTIVENESS AS A LEADER COMES FROM WHO YOU ARE, NOT WHAT YOU DO

have we spent debating and discussing the core and nuances of leadership? How many examples of leadership success and failure have we shared? I will forever be thankful for your influence on The Leadership Tree and *Who* Not What*. Every client with whom I interact is being influenced by the two of you.

This leaves only the most important leader for whom I've ever worked, **Mike Kane**. Mike, your transparency was a blazing example to me of what a secure, healthy leader can be. And your personal investment in me was enormous. Few people on the planet will ever have the privilege of following a more capable, well-developed person than you. There is no thanks big enough personally or professionally to cover what you have meant in my life and work.

No endeavor such as this is taken on without investment by one's family. In my case that is my wife, **Sarah**, and my kids, **Canon, Suri, Braxton,** and **Ayla**. All of you have, by proxy, joined me in the adventure to fulfill a calling to share important leadership messages with the world. Unfortunately, you see and feel, more than anyone else, the gaps between the great leadership I speak about and who I actually am. I hope to close that gap over the years.

Sarah, I am thankful to be married to a woman who is as smart, giving, talented, and willing to fight for a great marriage as you are. You are a wise advisor. You are special and specially made. "You are worth it!" and worth fighting for. (P.S. You're also stunningly beautiful.) Canon, Suri, Braxton, and Ayla, you have already blessed me beyond what I imagined having children would do. I hope I can become the leader God intended me to be for you.

Lastly, I choose to publicly thank **God** and the savior of my life and soul, **Jesus Christ**. I know in many circles it is somewhat fashionable to acknowledge God in a very general way these days. And yet I hesitated to acknowledge God in this thank you—not because I'm embarrassed by my faith, but because some people may choose not to listen to the leadership message I steward because of my beliefs. That, I think, would be sad, as the truths I've shared in this book apply to us all, regardless of our beliefs. That said, I choose to publicly offer my thanks to You, God, for igniting in me, on a single night in St. Louis in 1999, a passion for leadership. In a moment, You turned on a switch that has never turned off. You have given deep purpose to this work. Though the work I pursue is important, it will never be as important as You, the One who created everything. I am eternally thankful for Your guidance, presence, sacrifice, forgiveness, power, grace, and love.

Tim Spiker

The goal is to turn data into information,
and information into insight.

CARLY FIORINA

ENDNOTES + APPENDIX

The web references in this book were live and correct on May 25, 2020, but may be subject to change.

CHAPTER ONE: YOU ALREADY KNOW

1. If I ever share a story that is *based* on a true story, I explicitly state as much. I do it just once in this book: the story of Greg in Chapter 4 is based on a true story.

CHAPTER THREE: STUMBLING INTO SIGNIFICANCE

1. Based on knowledge and experience gained after these categories were initially created, some terminology has been modified to more accurately reflect reality as I understand it today.

2. Winzenburg, Vanessa, "Maximize Your Leadership Potential," *FMI Quarterly*, Issue 3, 2008, 24, https://www.fminet.com/wp-content/uploads/2016/12/2008_3_whole_issue.pdf.

3. Adapted from ibid.

4. "Measuring the Return on Character," *Harvard Business Review,* April 2015, https://hbr.org/2015/04/measuring-the-return-on-character.

5. Fred Kiel, Return on Character: *The Real Reason Leaders and Their Companies Win* (Boston: Harvard Business Review Press, 2015), 133.

6. KRW's study began with 121 companies but was ultimately narrowed to the 44 companies for which they had complete data sets. Their

data tracked these companies for two years. For some people the smaller company sample size and relatively short duration of the study might be a deterrent to leaning into KRW's findings. I disagree, which is why I cite their work. There are two realities that make KRW's findings worth paying attention to: (1) Their data found a statistically significant result through a vetted process. They could not have published their findings in any journal of note, most especially the *Harvard Business Review,* if their process and findings were not scientifically sound. (2) KRW adheres to a causality model of financial performance that identifies leadership as a 30% contributor to final financial results. Macroeconomic realities and the business model of the companies they study account for the remaining 70%. This means that KRW takes into account other factors besides leadership in assessing the financial results of the companies they studied. Therefore, it would not be accurate to suggest that KRW's results were skewed by non-leadership factors. For these two reasons, I believe that, despite the small sample size and short duration of the study, KRW's findings are valuable and worth noting. If you have concerns regarding a lack of explanation of causality in a study such as this, I offer Chapter Eight of this book as an explanation on the causality between the inner development of the leader and the production of results.

7.   "Measuring the Return on Character," ibid.

8.   Ibid.

9.   Human Synergistics Australia, *Why Leadership and Culture Matter—Proving the People and Performance Connection* (Australia: Human Synergistics International, 2014), 17. As a side note, those that employ the "most Constructive Styles" not only excel in being constructive but are also very low in less effective styles, which Human Synergistics calls Defensive Styles—Passive Defensive and Aggressive Defensive.

10.   Leadership/Impact® aimed at senior executives, developed by Dr. Robert A. Cooke, and Management/Impact® aimed at middle managers, developed by Dr. Janet Szumal. Each of these produced additional data pointing to a positive relationship between

Constructive Styles and leadership effectiveness. Data from the Leadership/Impact calculated that leaders who most exemplified Constructive Styles outperformed leaders who least exemplified Constructive Styles on average by 23%. Data from the Management/Impact calculated that leaders who most exemplified Constructive Styles outperformed leaders who least exemplified Constructive Styles on average by 36%. These statistics can be found in *Why Leadership and Culture Matter – Proving the People and Performance Connection*, 31 and 51.

11. Adapted from ibid.

12. Each LSI survey filled out about a leader (known as a "focal manager"), including the leader's self-evaluation, counted as a data point. With an average of 8 responders per leader assessed, Human Synergistics International Group has had more than 250,000 leaders take the LSI, resulting in over 2 million data points.

CHAPTER FOUR: CHASM AND CONNECTION

1. I've modified some of the language in this book from the leadership model that was used in the original 360 leadership assessment. This is what I was referring to in endnote #1 from Chapter 3. Let me explain further.

   The original language in the model was authored quite intentionally to indicate that the eight leadership categories were things that leaders did. They were actions and behaviors they took—"Behaviors and Skills of Leadership" as they were referred to. The categories of Inwardly Sound and Others Focused weren't in the original model. Instead, Inwardly Sound was "Lead Within" and Others Focused was "Focus on Others."

   This might be the time where you find yourself saying, "Tim, I think you're about to drown me in detail. Why does any of this matter?" I'm glad you asked.

   I've changed them after the epiphany moment I described in the Introduction, because when you look at what lives inside each of these two areas, you quickly find concepts that dive deeper than mere actions. The substance of these two areas lives in the psyche, attitude, ego, character, and motives of every leader surveyed by those 360s. Action-oriented language alone couldn't fully account for them. The language of "Lead Within" and "Focus on Others" in the original model was inaccurate. That inaccurate language, which I was chiefly responsible for creating, was a major reason it took years for me to see the reality of *Who* Not What* after the research data had been analyzed. (How's that for irony?)

So to save everyone else the years of contemplation I went through, I've changed the terminology in this book to more accurately reflect reality. "Lead Within" becomes "Inwardly Sound." "Focus on Others" becomes "Others Focused." This new language now intentionally reflects who leaders are as people rather than what they do as leaders. As I share in this chapter, this is a critical distinction from seeing and teaching leadership as merely behaviors and skills.

I didn't put this text in the main body of the book because I expected that only the nerdiest of leadership nerds would care or be interested in this. If you read this endnote and enjoyed it, welcome to the LNC, the Leadership Nerds Club.

2. This story is based on a real-life event with some expansion of the details based on my consulting experience and business observations.

3. The Leadership Tree has been developed in conjunction with John Ott and Vanessa Kiley (exceptionalleaders.com).

4. During off-site leader development experiences, I've found this definition of manipulation is disturbingly close to the most common answer people give when asked what they want to learn about leadership. They often say, "I want to learn how to get my people to execute my ideas without realizing they're doing it." Yikes!

CHAPTER FIVE: DEFINING WHAT IT MEANS TO BE INWARDLY SOUND

1. Who* Not What™, Who Not What™, W*NW™, WNW™, Inwardly Sound™, Others Focused™, and Outwardly Focused™ are

trademarks of The Aperio and Tim Spiker. All rights reserved.

2. David Zes and Dana Landis, "A Better Return on Self-Awareness," The Korn/Ferry Institute, August 2013, 1, https://www.kornferry. com/content/dam/kornferry/docs/article-migration/KFI-SelfAwareness-ProofPoint-6.pdf.

3. Tasha Eurich, "What Self-Awareness Really Is (and How to Cultivate It)," *Harvard Business Review*, January 4, 2018, https://hbr. org/2018/01/what-self-awareness-really-is-and-how-to-cultivate-it.

4. Fabio Sala, "Executive Blind Spots: Discrepancies Between Self- and Other-Ratings," *Consulting Psychology Journal Practice and Research*, 55(4):222-229, September 2003, https://www.researchgate. net/publication/232559373_Executive_Blind_Spots_Discrepancies_ Between_Self-_and_Other-Ratings.

5. Jennifer Pittman, "Speaking Truth to Power: The Role of the Executive," Markkula Center for Applied Ethics at Santa Clara University, https://www.scu.edu/ethics/focus-areas/business-ethics/ resources/speaking-truth-to-power-the-role-of-the-executive/.

6. Eurich, ibid.

7. Cheryl Armon and Theo L. Dawson, "Developmental Trajectories in Moral Reasoning Across the Life Span," *Journal of Moral Education*, Volume 26, No. 4, 1997, 433-453, https://dts.lectica.org/PDF/ Trajectories.pdf.

8. Researcher Lawrence Kohlberg of Harvard University is a well-cited psychologist whose work supports the development of ethics in adults through formal education. His research was furthered by James Rest. For a short article from Santa Clara University's Manuel Velasquez, Claire Andre, Thomas Shanks, S.J., and Michael J. Meyer, describing Rest's conclusions in response to a Wall Street Journal article suggesting ethics could not be taught, go to https://legacy.scu.edu/ ethics/publications/iie/v1n1/taught.html.

9. Jonathon D. Brown, "Understanding the Better Than Average Effect: Motives (Still) Matter," *Personality and Social Psychology Bulletin*, 38(2), 209-219, http://faculty.washington.edu/jdb/articles/Brown%20 (2012,%20PSPB,%20motives).pdf.

10. Lenny Bernstein, "A growing body of evidence links exercise and mental acuity," *The Washington Post,* May 25, 2010, http://www.washingtonpost.com/wp-dyn/content/article/2010/05/24/AR2010052402608.html.

11. Healthline, "12 Science-Based Benefits of Meditation," https://www.healthline.com/nutrition/12-benefits-of-meditation.

12. MagnifyMoney, "21% of Divorcées Cite Money as the Cause of Their Divorce, MagnifyMoney Survey Shows," https://www.magnifymoney.com/blog/featured/money-causes-21-percent-divorces925885150/.

13. Lauren M. Papp, E. Mark Cummings, and Marcie C. Gokey-Morey, "For Richer, for Poorer: Money as a Topic of Marital Conflict in the Home," Family Relations: Interdisciplinary Journal of Applied Family Science, 58(1), February 2009, 91-103, https://onlinelibrary.wiley.com/doi/full/10.1111/j.1741-3729.2008.00537.x.

CHAPTER SIX: DEFINING WHAT IT MEANS TO BE OTHERS FOCUSED

1. Parker J. Palmer, "The Gift of Presence, The Perils of Advice," On Being blog, https://onbeing.org/blog/the-gift-of-presence-the-perils-of-advice.

2. "Our Leadership Team: Bob Chapman," https://www.barrywehmiller.com/our-business/leadership-team/bob-chapman.

3. Bob Chapman and Raj Sisodia, *Everybody Matters: The Extraordinary Power of Caring for Your People Like Family* (New York: Portfolio / Penguin, 2015), 63-64.

4. I am forever indebted to consultant Dr. Mary Shippy (alignleadership.com) for teaching me this phrase. Not a week goes by in my life when I don't use it personally or share it with a leader.

5. William A. Gentry, Todd J. Weber, and Golnaz Sadri, "Empathy in the Workplace: A Tool for Effective Leadership," Center for

Creative Leadership, February 2016, https://www.ccl.org/wp-content/uploads/2015/04/EmpathyInTheWorkplace.pdf.

6.   Though too long to share in the body of this book, here in the endnotes I would like to share two specific quotes regarding humility from author C.S. Lewis.

The first comes from The Screwtape Letters, a fictional story about demons who work to oppose God's purposes in the lives of normal people. Therefore, where you see the term "patient" in the quote, it refers to the person the demons are working to keep separated from God.

"You must therefore conceal from the patient the true end of Humility. Let him think of it not as self-forgetfulness but as a certain kind of opinion (namely, a low opinion) of his own talents and character. Some talents, I gather, he really has. Fix in his mind the idea that humility consists in trying to believe those talents to be less valuable than he believes them to be. No doubt they are in fact less valuable than he believes, but that is not the point. The great thing is to make him value an opinion for some quality other than truth, thus introducing an element of dishonesty and make-believe into the heart of what otherwise threatens to become a virtue. By this method thousands of humans have been brought to think that humility means pretty women trying to believe they are ugly and clever men trying to believe they are fools. And since what they are trying to believe may, in some cases, be manifest nonsense, they cannot succeed in believing it and we have the chance of keeping their minds endlessly revolving on themselves in an effort to achieve the impossible. To anticipate the Enemy's strategy, we must consider His aims. The Enemy wants to bring the man to a state of mind in which he could design the best cathedral in the world, and know it to be the best, and rejoice in the fact, without being any more (or less) or otherwise glad at having done it than he would be if it had been done by another. The Enemy wants him, in the end, to be so free from any bias in his own favour that he can rejoice in his own talents as frankly and gratefully as in his neighbour's talents—or in a sunrise, an elephant, or a waterfall."

C.S. Lewis, *The Screwtape Letters* (New York: HarperOne, 2015), 70-71.

"Do not imagine that if you meet a really humble man he will be what most people call 'humble' nowadays: he will not be a sort of greasy, smarmy person, who is always telling you that, of course, he is nobody. Probably all you will think about him is that he seemed a cheerful, intelligent chap who took a real interest in what you said to him. If you do dislike him it will be because you feel a little envious of anyone who seems to enjoy life so easily. He will not be thinking about humility: he will not be thinking about himself at all."

C.S. Lewis, *Mere Christianity* (New York: HarperOne, 2015), 128.

7. Lewis, The Screwtape Letters, 70.

8. Rick Howard and Jamie Lash, *This Was Your Life!: Preparing to Meet God Face to Face* (Grand Rapids: Baker, 1998), 85.

9. Depending on what school of thought and research to which you ascribe, the Ancient Greeks identified and had different words for between four and eight different types of "love."

10. Another potentially helpful definition to consider comes from FMI (FMInet.com), the consulting firm for whom I formerly worked. They defined agapeo—just a different form of the verb from agapone—as "Doing what's in the best interest of others, with or without their knowledge, consistently over time, unconditionally."

11. R. K. Greenleaf, *The Servant as Leader* (Atlanta: Greenleaf Publishing Center, 1970).

12. Matt Crossman, "Forever Herb," *Southwest: The Magazine,* March 2019, https://www.southwestmag.com/herb-kelleher/.

13. "Company Reports," http://investors.southwest.com/financials/company-reports/annual-reports.

14. "Southwest Airlines Announces Succession Transition Plan," https://www.swamedia.com/releases/release-b6eb9175c8e5b718790a204c4b705645?lang=en-US

15. Leah MarieAnne Klett, "Southwest Airlines: How faith, servant leadership of Colleen Barrett led to company's massive success," The Christian Post, January 12, 2019, https://www.christianpost.com/news/southwest-airlines-how-faith-servant-leadership-of-colleen-

barrett-led-to-companys-massive-success.html.

16. Ibid.

17. Eva Rykrsmith, "What Is Servant Leadership? Thoughts from Southwest Airlines President, Colleen Barrett," QuickBase, September 20, 2010, https://www.quickbase.com/blog/what-is-servant-leadership-thoughts-from-southwest-airlines-president-colleen-barrett

18. "World's Most Admired Companies," *Fortune*, http://fortune.com/worlds-most-admired-companies/

19. Southwest Airlines, "Company Reports," http://investors.southwest.com/financials/company-reports/annual-reports.

20. Towers Watson, "2012 Global Workforce Study," 9, https://employeeengagement.com/wp-content/uploads/2012/11/2012-Towers-Watson-Global-Workforce-Study.pdf

21. Ibid.

22. Purdue University Sports, "2017-18 Purdue Men's Basketball Media Guide," 196, https://s3.amazonaws.com/purduesports.com/documents/2017/10/15/_pur_m_baskbl_2017_18_misc_non_event__18-mbb-mediaguide.pdf.

23. https://www.woodenaward.com/2007_recipient_gene_keady.

24. Travis Baugh, "Keady 'humbled and happy' to reach Hall of Fame," *The Exponent,* April 3, 2012, http://www.purdueexponent.org/sports/article_07e3e495-f596-5a66-b72c-8f7aadb2bc94.html?mode=story.

25. Associated Press, "Keady, Massimino to join Hall," ESPN, April 1, 2013, http://espn.go.com/mens-college-basketball/story/_/id/9122617/gene-keady-rollie-massimino-headline-hall-fame-class.

26. Linc Darner: Green Bay (2015–2020); Alan Major: Charlotte (2010–2015), Cuonzo Martin: Missouri (2017–present), Cal (2014–2017), Tennessee (2011–2014), Missouri State (2008–2011); Matt Painter: Purdue (2005–present), Southern Illinois (2003–2004); Bruce Weber: Kansas State (2012–present), Illinois (2003–2012), Southern Illinois (1998–2003).

27. Given that this is a rather serious book, it might seem strange

to dedicate an endnote to Gene Keady's hairstyle. But given the relationship between insecurity and leadership effectiveness and the rather amazing amount of attention Keady's hairstyle has received over the years, it is something worth addressing.

One of the most often ridiculed aspects of Gene Keady was his hair. He had a weave/comb-over that seemed to scream from the top of its lungs, "Coach is not going to admit he's lost his hair . . . no matter what!" This quirk in Keady's personal style seems to contradict the idea that he was a secure person. After all, why would someone who was comfortable in his own skin go to such lengths to hide a relatively normal physical attribute that simply couldn't be hidden? Answer: Keady was style challenged, not insecure.

In late 2014, multiple articles ran across the country as Keady came clean about his hair. He had finally cut it and then admitted to the press that he previously had extensions woven in with what little of his own hair was left. Though some may find it difficult to believe, Keady's comments showed that he previously thought his hairstyle was attractive. Keady said, "I thought I looked gorgeous with the comb-over."

Keady lost his sweet wife, Pat, to cancer in 2009. In 2013 he married again and his new wife, Kathleen Petrie, had a different view of Coach's hairstyle choice. "Coach thought it was pretty dapper," Kathleen told the Indianapolis Star. "I think it was horrible. I mean, it was really weird-looking. . . . And he's already so stern-looking. But with that hairdo, it was like Halloween or something." It seems her opinion has rubbed off on Coach. He now says, "Of course, it [the comb-over] was ugly."

Keady's hairstyle did not, as some might suppose, indicate the presence of significant personal insecurities that could undermine his effectiveness as a leader. It simply showed that none of us should go to him for fashion advice.

Quote from: "Gene Keady talks 'ugly' comb-over," ESPN, November 11, 2014, http://espn.go.com/mens-college-basketball/story/_/id/11860282/former-purdue-coach-gene-keady-talks-famous-comb-over.

28. Big Ten Conference 2019-20 Men's Basketball Media Guide, 86,

https://bigten.org/documents/2019/9/26/2019_20_Media_Guide_
FINAL.pdf.

29. Keady's care for us as people, not merely as basketball players while
we were on the team, was not limited to my own experience and
perception. When Keady was inducted into the National Collegiate
Basketball Hall of Fame in 2013, Purdue Athletic Director Morgan
Burke said of Keady's induction, "It reinforces his philosophy of
caring about individual student-athletes, both while they were here
and after they'd moved on from Purdue."

Quote from: Travis Baugh, "Former coach Gene Keady elected
to College Basketball Hall of Fame," *The Exponent,* April 2,
2013, https://www.purdueexponent.org/sports/mens/basketball/
article_6fdc9ff4-9b36-11e2-8c7d-001a4bcf6878.html.

CHAPTER SEVEN: ONE MORE THING

1. In the very last week (literally) of research for this book, I ran across
a definition of emotional intelligence that was eerily similar to the
definition of emotional maturity in this book. It comes from the
book *Executive EQ* by Dr. Robert K. Cooper and Ayman Sawaf. It
reads, "Emotional intelligence is the ability to sense, understand, and
effectively apply the power and acumen of emotions as a source of
human energy, information, connection, and influence." [Dr. Robert
K. Cooper and Ayman Sawaf, *Executive EQ: Emotional Intelligence
in Leadership and Organizations,* (New York: Berkly Publishing
Group, 1997), xiii.]

I have no recollection of seeing this definition from Cooper and Sawaf
previously. But the similarities are too close to ignore. It is my best
guess that those who have influenced me in my understanding and
definition of what it means to be emotionally mature were consciously
or unconsciously influenced by the definition authored by Cooper
and Sawaf. Thus, I include a note here referencing their work even
though the two definitions aren't identical and I have no recollection
of reading their work.

2. "Emotional Intelligence," http://www.danielgoleman.info/topics/emotional-intelligence/.

3. CEOs and their top management team: Sigal G. Barsade, Andrew J. Ward, et al. "To Your Heart's Content: A Mode of Affective Diversity in Top Management Teams," *Administrative Science Quarterly,* 45 (2000): 802–836.

4. Daniel Goleman, Richard Boyatzis, and Annie McKee, *Primal Leadership: Unleashing the Power of Emotional Intelligence* (Boston: Harvard Business Review Press, 2013), 14-15.

5. Leaders as the managers of meaning: Howard Gardner, *Leading Minds: An Anatomy of Leadership* (New York: Basic Books, 1995).

6. Goleman, Boyatzis, and McKee, 8-9.

7. Six Seconds, "Why 'Six Seconds' – About Our Intriguing Name," https://www.6seconds.org/2019/06/19/why-six-seconds-about-our-intriguing-name/.

8. Thank you to Dr. Mary Shippy (alignleadership.com) for teaching me this analogy.

CHAPTER EIGHT: A MATTER OF TRUST

1. Simon Sinek, *Leaders Eat Last Deluxe: Why Some Teams Pull Together and Others Don't* (New York: Penguin, 2017), 16.

2. The Relationship Between Engagement at Work and Organizational Outcomes 2016 Q12® Meta-Analysis: Ninth Edition, 2, http://www.workcompprofessionals.com/advisory/2016L5/august/MetaAnalysis_Q12_ResearchPaper_0416_v5_sz.pdf.

3. Gallup, *2016 State of the Global Workforce* (Washington, D.C.: Gallup Press, 2017), 4-5, https://www.gallup.com/workplace/238079/state-global-workplace-2017.aspx.

4. https://www.ddiworld.com/DDIWorld/media/monographs/employeeengagement_mg_ddi.pdf?ext=.pdf, 1, Developmental Dimensions International (DDI) found only 19% of employees were

highly engaged. In its report, DDI cited research from The Corporate Executive Board and Towers Watson (known as Towers Perrin at the time of their report) which found that only 11% and 17%, respectively, of employees are highly engaged.

5. Gallup, *2016 State of the Global Workforce*, 22-24.

6. Gallup, *2016 State of the American Workforce* (Washington, D.C.: Gallup Press, 2017), 61, https://www.gallup.com/workplace/238085/state-american-workplace-report-2017.aspx

7. Ibid., 71.

8. Gallup, *2016 State of the Global Workforce*, 40.

9. Interaction Associates, "Building Workplace Trust: Trends and High Performance," 2014, 17.

10. "2019 *Fortune* 100 Best Trends: Employee Experience at the Best Workplaces in America," Great Place to Work, 2019, 4, https://cloud.kapostcontent.net/pub/0204ea80-c203-4933-a13a-bf13041f0531/2019-fortune-100-best-trends-employee-experience-at-the-best-workplaces-in-america-2?kui=b1Rhivmc8GS3wtL1cal2Eg.

11. 2.95 times that of the Russell 1000 and 2.92 times that of the Russell 3000. https://www.greatplacetowork.com/images/reports/Fortune_100_Report_2017_FINAL.pdf, 6.

12. McKinsey & Company is broadly regarded as the world's most prestigious management consulting firm. At the time of publication of this book, McKinsey has more than 30,000 employees based in 130 countries. McKinsey counts CEO's of numerous multinational corporations among its alumni. McKinsey is known for its rigor and thoroughness therefore its research is trusted globally. You can read more about McKinsey at www.McKinsey.com.

13. https://www.mckinsey.com/solutions/orgsolutions/overview/organizational-health-index

14. Ibid.

CHAPTER NINE: MYTHS AND MISUNDERSTANDINGS

1. Inhelder, B. & Piaget, J. (1958) *The Growth of Logical Thinking from Childhood to Adolescence* (New York, Basic Books, Inc.). For a quick reference on Piaget's work, go to https://www.simplypsychology.org/piaget.html. For a short video about Piaget's work, go to https://www.youtube.com/watch?v=IhcgYgx7aAA.

2. Chapter 5, page 77.

3. Armon and Dawson, "Developmental Trajetories," 433-453.

4. Kohlberg, L. (1981) *The Philosophy of Moral Development* (New York, Harper & Row). For a quick reference on Kohlberg's work, go to https://www.simplypsychology.org/kohlberg.html. For a short video about Kohlberg's work, go to https://www.youtube.com/watch?v=bounwXLkme4.

5. Armon and Dawson, "Developmental Trajetories," 436-437, 444.

6. Chapter 8, pages 165-167.

7. Soyoung Kim and Poornima Gupta, "Jobs abrasive style drove some people away — biographer," Reuters.com, October 23, 2011, https://www.reuters.com/article/apple-jobs/jobs-abrasive-style-drove-some-people-away-biographer-idUSN1E79K1SL20111024.

8. Brent Schlender and Rick Tetzeli, *Becoming Steve Jobs: The Evolution of a Reckless Upstart into a Visionary Leader* (New York: Crown Business, 2016).

9. To learn more about our tendency to give ourselves the benefit of the doubt while not doing so for others, investigate psychology's "Fundamental Attribution Error." Here's a place you can start: http://www.psychologytoday.com/blog/real-men-dont-write-blogs/201406/why-we-dont-give-each-other-break.

10. Big thanks to my wife, Sarah, for teaching me this phrase and, more importantly, the sentiment behind it.

11. Jim Collins, *Good to Great: Why Some Companies Make the Leap and Others Don't* (New York: HarperCollins, 2001).

12. Collins, 63.

CHAPTER TEN: TWO FOR THE SHOW

1. Patrick Lencioni, *The Advantage: Why Organizational Health Trumps Everything Else in Business* (San Francisco: Jossey-Bass, 2012), 1, 3.

TABLES AND FIGURES

SPECIAL CODES

Special Code #1: dki897ej
Special Code #2: slo987w2
Special Code #3: rp0782hx
Special Code #4: 98uhy5s8
Special Code #5: ccd23wef
Special Code #6: xad458hh
Special Code #7: 34erdf6y
Special Code #8: 09oki87y
Special Code #9: 6789iku7
Special Code #10: ghd4532w
Special Code #11: 47yhf76e
Special Code #12: 4h4y6r78
Special Code #13: 37dygt54
Special Code #14: 44ry88oi
Special Code #15: aq125mj7
Special Code #16: aju57fh2

THE LEADERSHIP TREE

THE WHAT OF LEADERSHIP

PURSUE VISION

DRIVE CULTURE

THINK STRATEGICALLY

MARSHAL RESOURCES

ENSURE EXECUTION

CULTIVATE TALENT

UNLEASH MOTIVATION

COMMUNICATE EFFECTIVELY

THE WHO OF LEADERSHIP

OTHERS FOCUSED

INWARDLY SOUND

*3/4 OF YOUR EFFECTIVENESS AS A LEADER COMES FROM WHO YOU ARE, NOT WHAT YOU DO

THE WHO OF LEADERSHIP

OTHERS FOCUSED

ATTENTIVE

CURIOUS

EMPATHIC

HUMBLE

AGAPONE (ἀγαπῶν)

EMOTIONALLY MATURE

INWARDLY SOUND

SECURE + SETTLED

SELF-AWARE

PRINCIPLED

HOLISTICALLY HEALTHY

PURPOSEFUL

THE ONLY LEADERS WORTH* FOLLOWING

ATTENTIVE

OTHERS FOCUSED

BEING FULLY PRESENT TO AND
FULLY ENGAGED WITH OTHERS
IN EVERY INTERACTION

CURIOUS

OTHERS FOCUSED

(A) PROACTIVELY SEEKING GREATER
UNDERSTANDING OF PEOPLE AND SITUATIONS

("Understanding" is not merely intellectual curiosity limited
to facts—it includes the perspectives and emotions of others.)

— OR —

(B) LIVING LIFE WITH A PROACTIVE BIAS
AGAINST THE ACT OF ASSUMING

*3/4 OF YOUR EFFECTIVENESS AS A LEADER COMES FROM WHO YOU ARE, NOT WHAT YOU DO

EMPATHIC

OTHERS FOCUSED

STANDING IN OTHERS' SHOES LONG ENOUGH TO
STEP 1   UNDERSTAND THEIR PERSPECTIVES,
STEP 2   FEEL WHAT THEY FEEL, AND
STEP 3   EXPRESS THOSE FEELINGS BACK TO THEM

HUMBLE

OTHERS FOCUSED

HAVING A MINDSET OF SELF-FORGETFULNESS,
A WILLINGNESS TO SEE AND ADMIT FAULT,
AND AN EAGERNESS TO ACKNOWLEDGE OTHERS

AGAPONE (ἀγαπῶν)

OTHERS FOCUSED

SERVICE TO AND CARE FOR OTHERS THAT IS
SELFLESS, CONSISTENT, AND UNCONDITIONAL

EMOTIONALLY MATURE

INWARDLY SOUND AND OTHERS FOCUSED

RECOGNIZING AND RESPONDING TO MY EMOTIONS AND
THE EMOTIONS OF OTHERS IN WAYS THAT INCREASE
ENERGY, CONNECTION, INFLUENCE, AND INFORMATION[†]

†See Citation for Chapter 7, Endnote 1, Page 257.

*3/4 OF YOUR EFFECTIVENESS AS A LEADER COMES FROM WHO YOU ARE, NOT WHAT YOU DO

SECURE + SETTLED

INWARDLY SOUND

COMFORTABLE IN MY OWN SKIN
AND AT PEACE ABOUT WHAT
THE FUTURE MAY BRING

SELF-AWARE

INWARDLY SOUND

AN ACCURATE AND REASONABLE UNDERSTANDING OF
WHO I AM—MY STRENGTHS, WEAKNESSES, QUIRKS,
PREFERENCES, HOT BUTTONS, PERSONALITY STYLE, DENTS,
AND WORLDVIEW—AND HOW WHO I AM AFFECTS OTHERS

PRINCIPLED

INWARDLY SOUND

COURAGEOUS	MOVE FORWARD IN THE FACE OF FEAR.
HONEST	ASCERTAIN THE TRUTH CAREFULLY AND COMMUNICATE IT ACCURATELY.
AUTHENTIC	GENUINELY SHARE HOW I THINK, WHAT I FEEL, AND WHO I AM.
INTEGRITY	DO WHAT I SAY I WILL... AND PROACTIVELY ADMIT WHEN I DON'T.
GRIT	LEVERAGE MENTAL FORTITUDE TO PRODUCE COMMITMENT AND DETERMINATION.

HOLISTICALLY HEALTHY

INWARDLY SOUND

RESILIENCE AND CAPACITY IN EACH AREA OF LIFE:
PHYSICAL, FINANCIAL, INTELLECTUAL, VOCATIONAL,
MENTAL, EMOTIONAL, RELATIONAL, AND SPIRITUAL

*3/4 OF YOUR EFFECTIVENESS AS A LEADER COMES FROM WHO YOU ARE, NOT WHAT YOU DO

PURPOSEFUL

INWARDLY SOUND

BEING INTENTIONAL ABOUT HOW I AM
INVESTING MY LIFE AND LIVING IN ALIGNMENT
WITH WHAT IS MOST IMPORTANT TO ME

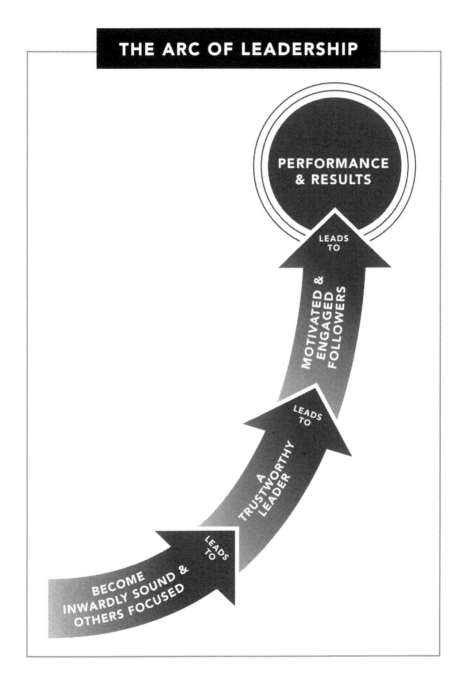

THE ARC OF LEADERSHIP

PERFORMANCE & RESULTS

LEADS TO

MOTIVATED & ENGAGED FOLLOWERS

LEADS TO

A TRUSTWORTHY LEADER

LEADS TO

BECOME INWARDLY SOUND & OTHERS FOCUSED

*3/4 OF YOUR EFFECTIVENESS AS A LEADER COMES FROM WHO YOU ARE, NOT WHAT YOU DO

Made in the USA
Las Vegas, NV
11 August 2021